THE GREAT BLACK SWAMP:

historical tales of 19th-century northwest ohio

photography & narrative by

JIM MOLLENKOPF

THE GREAT BLACK SWAMP

historical tales of 19th-century northwest ohio

photography & narrative by

JIM MOLLENKOPF

©1999 Lake of the Cat Publishing,
P.O. Box 351454, Toledo, Ohio, 43635-1454
All rights reserved.
ISBN 978-0-9665910-1-9
Library of Congress Catalog No. 99-073706

First Edition
Second printing, January 2000
Third printing, July 2000
Fourth printing, May 2001
Fifth printing, November 2002
Sixth printing, March 2004
Seventh printing, September 2005
Eighth printing, December 2007
Ninth printing, June 2013

DEDICATION:

To Denise

Table of Contents:

Table of Contents (continued)

List of Illustrations And Photographs

List of Illustrations
And Photographs (continued)

Map of Northwest Ohio, 1850. (Courtesy of Map Collection, University of Toledo Libraries.)

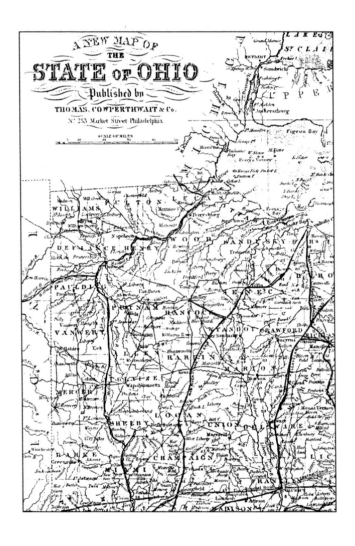

Foreword

On New Year's Day, 1800, northwest Ohio and the Maumee Valley looked little different than it had for thousands of years. While in other parts of Ohio forests were being turned into farmland and cities such as Cleveland, Columbus, and Cincinnati had taken root, the barrier presented by the Great Black Swamp had enveloped the area in sort of a temporary time warp.

Indians from as many as ten different tribes roamed the area and lived in their traditional ways. The delay in white settlement afforded them a few more precious years before they would begin dying from the white man's attrition or be sent west in exile.

After the War of 1812 battles in northwest Ohio in the spring and summer of 1813 swept the British and Indians from power, settlers from the young United States of America began to drift to the region. After about 1830 this drift turned into a flood with the hunger for land leading settlers to penetrate even the Great Black Swamp with its terrific mud, mosquitoes, and malaria.

The first few generations of settlers to northwest Ohio endured and left their stories behind, some of which are in this book. Their tales of hardships and heartbreak make the problems of modern life seem small.

Other stories in this book include one of the Shawnee Chief Tecumseh who spent some of the last days of his life in the region; of a Revolutionary War soldier who enjoyed the frontier isolation of the Maumee Valley; of some of the city of Toledo's early trials and tribulations; and of the author Charles Dickens who brushed by the area on a sight-seeing trip.

By New Year's Day, 1900, northwest Ohio and the Maumee Valley had undergone tremendous change. The Great Black Swamp had been drained and plowed into farmland, a half dozen cities, led by Toledo, had been established and were thriving, and the Indians were but an afterthought. The Fallen Timbers Monument pictured on the cover represents, from left to right, the transition the area underwent in the 19th century. The Native American was still dominant when the century started, the settler was dominant by its end, with the soldier in the middle, Anthony Wayne, representing the catalyst of that change, military force.

I would like to acknowledge all those involved in preserving northwest Ohio history including the local history departments at the Toledo-Lucas County Public Library, the Wood County Public Library in Bowling Green, and the local history collection at the University of Toledo. In addition the access the university provided to a statewide borrowing system was invaluable. Acknowledgment is also due to all those involved with the *Northwest Ohio Quarterly*, an historical journal since 1929, and a wealth of primary source and bibliographic information.

This book is meant to provide a glimpse of life, good and bad, as it was in 19th century northwest Ohio. While I strove for accuracy it should not be viewed as a text of historical reference. History by its very nature is filled with errors of fact and subjective interpretation, reflecting the fallibility of the humans who have gathered it. However, as the writer Anatole France once observed, "All the historical books which contain no lies are extremely tedious."

Chapter I:

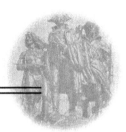

THE GREAT BLACK SWAMP

"My great terrour, the Black Swamp, is passed."

So wrote a man in 1815 in a letter to his wife after traveling from Fremont to Perrysburg through the heart of the Great Black Swamp. His attitude was typical of his day. For the Black Swamp, now an emerald quiltwork of highly productive farmland, was once a vast tract of marsh sweeping across northwest Ohio from the Lake Erie shore along the south side of the Maumee River to around Fort Wayne, Indiana. Ridges interrupted its horizontal tableau in places, sandy hills prowled by wolves and bears and darkened by the cathedral ceilings of towering trees.

The Black Swamp was probably so named by War of 1812 soldiers unlucky enough to have slogged across it. One soldier who became lost in it told his commander he had wandered into "the home of Satan." It spread over parts of 12 northwest Ohio counties including all of Wood and Paulding counties, the latter said to be the flattest one in Ohio. The cities of Sandusky, Fremont, Fostoria, Findlay, Defiance and Toledo roughly mark its onetime Ohio perimeter, with Bowling Green being the only city located wholly within it.

Water covered its surface for most of the year, save for the height of a dry summer or when frozen solid in a cold winter. Travel was almost impossible and what early roads were attempted soon sank into the quagmire, mud that could sink a horse to its chest.

Pioneers streaming west in the late 1700's and early 1800's detoured around northwest Ohio and the Black Swamp and it remained a pristine marshland, home to some Indians and a few hardy white hunters and traders. However around 1830, as much of the available land east of the Mississippi River had been snapped up, ambitious settlers began to carve out homesteads on ridges and river banks. The early arrivers paid a price.

Summer brought swarming clouds of mosquitoes and to ward them off settlers perspired in thick clothing, mittens, and headwraps, their poor horses similarly attired. Smoke hugged the ground in the evenings as smudge pots, lit to keep the mosquitoes away, made the settlers like so many hams in a smokehouse. And the nights were flooded with the baritone croaking of thousands of frogs, accented by the tenor sounds of howling wolves and screeching owls.

But the worst warm weather affliction was the dreaded ague, or swamp fever, which came in late summer and flattened its victims with soaring fever, deep chills, and violent shaking. A passer-by could tell by the sound of a rattling bed when a cabin's occupant had the dreaded disorder. Newcomers arriving in the Swamp were greeted with the observation, "there's someone we can divide the shakes with."

One historical observer characterized the Swamp as "perhaps no other more unhealthy place upon the whole continent than at this point of Wood and Lucas Counties." And in 1837 a Maumee resident was moved to poetry that went in part:

> "On Maumee, on Maumee,
> Tis ague in the fall;
> The fit will shake them so,
> It rocks the house and all.
> There's a funeral every day,
> Without a hearse or pall;
> They tuck them in the ground,
> With breeches, coat and all."

As fall cooled into winter, the settlers got a respite from ague and mosquitoes, merely to cope with the assorted hardships of long, cold and dark months spent in a remote, frontier setting. In spring hope sprang eternal, along with epic amounts of water and mud brought by rain and melting snows. Many early settlers gave up and left, their abandoned cabins mute monuments to the limits of human endurance. And one Wood County pioneer was allegedly murdered by his wife for refusing to take her out of the Swamp.

But the settlers kept coming for there was land to be had and dreams to be realized, even if that land they dreamed about lay under water most of the year. They were determined to wage war against the Swamp and win. Trees were felled, wild animals were killed off, and drainage projects were undertaken in earnest.

Draining an area the size of the Black Swamp, however, proved to be easier said than done and a hodgepodge of early efforts accomplished little. Eventually a series of "ditch laws" were passed and by around 1860 significant portions of the Swamp had been drained or were in the process of being so. One thing instrumental in the drainage efforts were clay tiles made from the clay subsoil of the Swamp itself, and by the 1870's there were over a dozen tile factories in the Black Swamp counties.

As the 19th century drew to a close, the majority of the Black Swamp lands had been drained and its rich, black soil turned into productive farmland. The flatness of the land was no longer interrupted by towering trees but by barns and grain silos. The "terrour" that was the Swamp had become a lush garden.

If the Great Black Swamp was still in existence today it probably would be a nature preserve and wildlife refuge similar to the Everglades in Florida. The only physical remnants of it are the Lake Erie marshes in eastern Lucas and western Ottawa counties. There areas such as Magee Marsh, the Ottawa National Wildlife Refuge, and Metzger Marsh preserve what once was the Swamp's northern edge.

Deep drainage ditches that line many roads in the Black Swamp counties, some big enough to swallow an automobile,

serve as a reminder of the effort it took to drain the Swamp.
And after a period of heavy rain the standing water left in Black
Swamp farm fields recalls, if only on a small scale, the great
marsh that's now part of northwestern Ohio lore.

Magee Marsh State Nature Reserve in Ottawa
County preserves a small part of what was once
the Great Black Swamp. Flat, marshy plains in-
terrupted by ridges with tall trees characterized
the majority of the Swamp's terrain.

Chapter II:

FROM SCOTLAND TO PERRYSBURG

Immigrants streamed by the millions from Europe to America in the 19th century, leaving behind families, friends, and all that was familiar for a long voyage to a distant land. Here they built new lives with their blood, sweat, and tears.

Most of their stories went unrecorded, anonymous weaves in the tapestry of human endeavor. However the story of Robert Fenton who came to Wood County from Scotland in 1834 lives on. He told his story in a speech given in Bowling Green in 1883 and his words were recorded in an historical text.

When Fenton was a boy his family, along with a group of fellow Scotsmen and their clans, left the city of Glasgow in April of 1834. Their destination was Perrysburg and the Great Black Swamp lands south of the city still available for settlement. They boarded a "little brig" that seemed far too small to sail the Atlantic, but sail they did.

The pounding 42-day voyage that followed left young Fenton's father much time to worry about his situation. For he was a shoemaker who had barely worked out-of-doors in his life, coming to a strange land with small children and a modest sum of money. After a rolling, seasick voyage the group landed in New York harbor. From there they traveled to Albany where the Erie Canal would provide passage to the city of Buffalo and Lake Erie.

Immigrants coming to America were an easy target for swindlers. One scheme common on the canal routes was for con artists to acquire a barely seaworthy boat and a broken down canal horse, collect large sums of money to take a group to their destination, then abandon the boat the first night, making off with the money. Many unwary canal-traveling immigrants arose from bed after the first night to the shock of stepping in cold water, their luggage floating and the boat sinking, its crooked operators long gone.

The Fenton entourage almost fell victim to such a swindle. After negotiating a passage to Buffalo with some "smooth-tongued Yankees," one of the group who had some seafaring experience noticed that the boat was in very poor condition and told the others to remove their luggage. "Now came the tug-of-war when we began to get our luggage ashore and the boatmen saw their plans to cheat us frustrated," Fenton recalled. Soon fists were flying and some blood was spilled. The boatmen swore out warrants and the head of each Scotch family was arrested. However they hired a lawyer and were cleared of the charges. "We thought this a pretty rough introduction to this land of promise."

The group charted passage with an honest operator and went on to Buffalo, amazed by the "monster snakes" they saw and the low roar of the bullfrogs they heard along the canal, things they had not seen or heard in Scotland. Once in Buffalo they took passage on an old steamer bound for Cleveland, a boat "that might have been built before the Revolution," and set sail.

On the way to Cleveland a German woman, mother of a large family, was drawing water from the lake with a bucket and fell overboard. The "rascally captain did not try to stop the boat which he could have done and perhaps saved the woman's life, but the heartless wretch actually wanted to know if the pail had been lost also. He seemed more concerned for the bucket than for the woman's life," Fenton recalled. "What happened to her poor orphan children I never learned, but their pitiful cries haunt me to this day."

Once in Cleveland they boarded a schooner "not finished or painted," to take them to the Maumee River and Perrysburg.

However after reaching Western Lake Erie it took the crew over half a day to find the mouth of the Maumee. The crew "knew no more about Perrysburg and the navigation of the Maumee than they did the course of the Nile," Fenton recollected.

The group finally reached the villages of Vistula and Port Lawrence, forerunners of the city of Toledo, where light winds brought their vessel to a stop. Quite impatient by now, the group took matters into their own hands and went ashore in what is now East Toledo. There they cut down trees, made some oars, and rowed the schooner upstream to Perrysburg. "I think this was the first vessel ever propelled up the Maumee River by the strong arms of a lot of sturdy Scotchmen," Fenton reminisced. They arrived in June, 1834.

The only house available for them was a partially completed cabin with no floor or doors, and cut outs in the walls for windows not yet installed. "With a few boards to put our chest on, four large families of us spent our first night in Perrysburg in this shelter on the 26th day of June, 1834." Fenton found work in a brickyard but after only nine days came down with swamp fever. "I recollect how terrified we were, not knowing anything of ague," he recalled. At one point 13 members of their group were so afflicted, laying prostrate in their crude shelter shaking with the trademark tremors of the disease.

As the summer wore on, members of the group began looking for land. Two of the family heads, Mr. Stewart and Mr. Davidson, went to Erie, PA to look at some property. On the way back, they stopped near Fremont for a drink of water and Mr. Davidson suddenly collapsed and died. A grief-stricken Mr. Stewart constructed a rough coffin and hired a team to transport his friend's body back to Perrysburg for burial, a difficult journey over poor roads.

"I shall never forget that awful, solemn evening when a wagon drove up to the house through the brush with the remains of Mr. Davidson," Fenton recalled. "I shall not attempt to describe that scene. Mrs. Davidson's situation and feelings with a family of small children, and in a land of strangers, can better be imagined than described."

In addition to death and disease, early hardships included wolves, which would howl outside the cabin doors at night, and raccoons which ate their crops. Another major hardship was the lack of a local mill which meant hauling their grain to the nearest mill in either Woodville or Waterville to be ground, nearly impossible to do in the winter. "I recollect nearly all one winter living wholly on potatoes," Fenton recalled. "The rest of our living was on corn meal, and that meal (was) made from frostbitten corn." Eventually they obtained a hand mill which allowed them to grind grain at home. The arrival of the hand mill was equivalent to seeing "the finest piano come into the house."

Most of the Scottish group eventually settled south of Perrysburg on land between that city and the Portage River. There was even a village named Fenton with a post office and a school on SR 199 (McCutchenville Road) near the intersection of Devil's Hole Road. However when the railroads came through Fenton was bypassed, and no trace of the village remains today. The village of Scotch Ridge, at the intersection of SR 199 and SR 105, and the Scottish graves in Webster Township Cemetery just north of town, remain as visible reminders of the Scottish pioneers of Robert Fenton's era.

In concluding his 1883 speech Fenton explained that, despite the hardships and the deprivations, the pioneers were able to maintain a positive attitude. "We were happy, since we all were on about a common level and the exigencies of the situation made us alert, active, and energetic. We had to be up and doing and we rather seemed to enjoy it."

Chapter III:

THE JOHN HUNT CHRONICLE

Author's note: John Hunt was one of the earlier white residents of the Maumee Valley. Born in Fort Wayne in 1798, he spent his adolescence in Detroit helping his older brother Henry run a trading post. There he became well-schooled in the ways of commerce and frontier life, dealing with pioneers, Indians, and both British and American soldiers during the War of 1812. In 1816 at the urging of his brother Henry, the 18-year-old Hunt came to Maumee, then a sparsely settled outpost at the edge of the Great Black Swamp, and established his own trading post.

He went on to enjoy considerable commercial and political success in his life, serving at various times as mayor of Maumee, state senator, Lucas County treasurer, and postmaster of Toledo. In 1867 a group of citizens interested in local history, realizing that Hunt was one of the few living links to the area's frontier past, asked him to write his memoirs detailing his early years in Maumee.

This proved to be an invaluable resource since there is so little recorded local history from that era. His manuscript, given to the Maumee Valley Pioneer Association, was lost however after the death of that group's president in 1937. But in 1965 a Toledo Trust employee cleaning out some old drawers discovered the manuscript. The association's late president once had an office in the Toledo Trust building.

The Maumee Valley Historical Society, descendant of the Pioneer Association, regained possession of the memoirs and painstakingly edited and validated the facts within it before publishing it in 1979. Thanks to their efforts Hunt's memoirs can tell tales once again. What follows is a collection of stories drawn from the John Hunt Memoirs. Direct quotations from Hunt's writings have retained his original misspellings and grammatical style. John Hunt died in 1877 and is buried in Forest Cemetery in Toledo. The complete, lengthy memoir of John Hunt is available through the Maumee Valley Historical Society.

A JOURNEY OF PERIL

Travel these days has it inconveniences such as delayed or canceled flights for the air traveler or construction delays on the highways for the motorist. John Hunt took a trip in early January, 1817 that featured a few inconveniences, ones that nearly cost him his life.

Hunt had been in Maumee only a few months, but the young man must have established a reputation for integrity during his years in Detroit as he had received a request from a Detroit bank to travel to Buffalo with a bank check for $20,000, cash it, and bring the money back to the bank in Detroit. Despite the wintry conditions, he set out from Maumee with three other men: Auchenbaugh, a mail carrier returning to Cleveland; Provost, a Frenchman; and Wyatt Hartshorn, a settler returning to his home in Ottawa County.

The first night was uneventful as they crossed the icy Maumee River and stayed with the Hawley family, then one of the few residents of Perrysburg. Their destination the next night was to be a house on the Portage River in what is now Elmore, Ohio. Hunt, confident he and his group could travel the 15 miles by mid-afternoon, left Perrysburg in the morning with no food or material with which to start a fire.

Slogging through the Great Black Swamp with only marked trees to guide them it began to snow hard with "the mud and water nearly up to our Saddle Skirts." The sun set and the four men were faced with a serious dilemma; a long, dark January night lost in a huge, freezing swamp with no food or shelter.

Wyatt Hartshorn, the man from Ottawa County, who was not used to such "pionier service" expressed great alarm as to how they would survive. "I told him I would shew him," Hunt wrote. "I tied my horse to the limb of the tree put my saddle against another tree found a chunk of wood which to place my feet, put my saddle blanket around me, pulled my furr cap over my eyes, leaned back against the tree and laughingly said I had gone to bed." Hartshorn was stunned that Hunt could make light of such a serious matter but the group huddled close and "sat all night, the monatoney of the occasion was only changed by the screach of an owl or the howl of the woolf."

The next day things would only get worse. The hungry and cold four got up at dawn and resumed their icy slogging. After a while the horses, trembling and cutting their legs on the ice, refused to move anymore. The group removed their saddles and bags and let the horses go, Hunt reluctantly losing his prized pony. Shortly after that the unfortunate Hartshorn sprained his ankle and could no longer walk. He begged the others not to leave him alone to die.

Hunt suggested that Provost, the Frenchman, stay with Hartshorn for the sum of $5.00, a decent sum of money in those days. Provost refused and Hunt proposed they hold a drawing with the loser staying even if he had to be tied up to do so. Suddenly Provost changed his mind figuring he could lose both the drawing and the $5.00. Hunt was greatly relieved for Provost's "words was far better than any music I have ever herd, for I would not have been hired to stay for five thousand dollars."

Hunt and Auchenbaugh "shook hands with the two we left and recommenced our loanly tramp" and soon came to the swollen Toussaint River. Here they had to wade through a watery floodplain just to reach the main body of the river to find a fallen tree to help them across. Soaked and freezing, the pair finally crawled ashore on the other side looking "more like half drowned coons." Now hypothermia was setting in as Auchenbaugh "drowsey and disinclined to talk," did not want to go on.

After some difficulty Hunt got Auchenbaugh on his feet and they continued. Darkness came and the two sat down on a log, lost, exhausted, and frozen. Hunt too now was about ready to give up. They had only sat a few minutes when suddenly they heard the barking of a dog. Hunt dragged Auchenbaugh to his feet and they soon discovered the banks of the swollen Portage River. On the other side was the house of the Harris family, their original destination. Both men began yelling into the wind but could be heard only by the dog which kept barking.

Inside, Mrs. Harris, worried the dog was barking at stranded travelers, insisted that her husband go out and check. He, being sure the dog was barking at wolves, had no interest in venturing out until she informed him there'd be no supper until he did.

Mr. Harris and a man friend staying with them crossed the river in a canoe and discovered the exhausted pair who literally threw themselves into the bottom of the boat. Saved now, they were taken to the cabin where Mrs. Harris fed them a meal of venison steak, roast potatoes, coffee, and biscuits. "If ever I enjoyed a meal it was on that occasion," Hunt recalled.

Badly frostbitten and barely able to walk, Hunt prevailed upon Harris to go back to find Hartshorn and Provost who by now probably figured their days were over. Early the next morning Harris and his man friend agreed and returned with the pair by sunset.

After a few days recuperation, the group headed for the settlement of Lower Sandusky, now Fremont. There Hunt bought the only horse available, an old Army pack horse left over from the War of 1812. "I had to give forty five dollars which at that time was considered double its value. I mounted this hard riding hard-bitten and broken down horse for Buffaloe." Hunt continued on to Buffalo alone, completing the journey in 10 days with no remarkable events reported save for a persistent northeast wind nipping at his face.

In Buffalo he cashed the $20,000 check, which was paid in one dollar bills, and decided to return to Detroit via sleigh through Canada as he was in no hurry to see the Great Black Swamp again anytime soon. As this route presented a different set of dangers, thieves, he hired a Captain Baird, sheriff of Niagara County, to accompany him. Hunt divided the money into two money belts, strapped one around his waist while Baird did the same with the other, and crossed the Niagara River into Canada.

The Canadian shore of Lake Erie was little more than a wild frontier in those days and, it being the dead of winter, accommodations would have to be taken where they could be found. They spent a comfortable first night in a pioneer home but were warned that the only accommodations that would be available the next night would be at a rough, roadside inn. There about 20 American deserters from the War of 1812 lived, men believed to be thieves and murderers who preyed on travelers.

When they arrived at the inn, out came the landlord, a man named Ward, accompanied by "20 of the roughest looking cases I ever saw," Hunt wrote. Captain Baird, who knew Ward, decided he would do the talking and told him they had no money and that he would pay for that night's stay upon his later return from Detroit.

The ruse seemed to work. However later in the evening Ward came up to Captain Baird, placed his hands upon his torso and felt the money belt. Captain Baird, who had been a quartermaster in the American Army in the War of 1812, explained that they were quartermaster documents left from the war that needed to be filed in Detroit. Ward seemed suspicious of the explanation but he left them alone.

Thus began a long night. Hunt and Captain Baird retired to "something they call a bed...a bundle of straw upon clapboards" and spent the night each with pistol in hand. The Americans at the inn began to drink heavily and get loud which could not have eased Hunt's and Captain Baird's nerves any. They decided that if attacked Captain Baird would shoot first and retreat behind Hunt and reload while Hunt opened fire.

They survived the night without being attacked. The American deserters drank all night "hooping and hollowing and dancing by the music of an old violin" and by dawn were deep in drunken slumber. Hunt and Captain Baird slipped quietly out of the inn and readied their sleigh for departure. They returned to pay Ward and saw a sight that "caped (capped) anything that I had ever seen in that way. The men and the old woman (Ward's wife) were laying strewed all over the floor with their Keg of whiskey in the midst."

Hunt and Captain Baird left and, despite fears of being waylaid in the woods, got away safely. Captain Baird later said that his reputation in Canada, where he was well known, and the fact that Hunt's brother had married into an established Canadian family, had saved them from being attacked and likely murdered considering the amount of money they had.

The pair reached Detroit and turned the money over to the bank where Hunt asked the bank directors not to send him on such another wintertime trip. He returned to Maumee a month and a day after he had left, still a lad of 18 but even more wise and experienced in the ways of frontier life. There he received a pleasant surprise; the horses that had been abandoned in the swamp had been found by Indians and his prized pony had been returned, emaciated but alive.

A CHILD SEES HISTORY

John Hunt's childhood years prior to living in Detroit were nomadic as his father was an Army colonel who served at a number of posts. His father was commander of Fort Wayne in Indiana in 1798 when Hunt was born there and the year 1806 found the Hunt family in Bellefontaine, Missouri, upriver from St. Louis, where Colonel Hunt had been sent to establish a fort.

In September of that year eight-year-old John Hunt was rolling a hoop along the bank of the Missouri River when floating down the river came some major players in American history. "I saw two or three bark canoes of Indians I supposed landing and immediately told my Father that there was some strange looking Indians at the landing that they had long beards and large flapped hats on," Hunt recalled.

The men in beards young Hunt had mistaken for Indians were none other than the voyagers Lewis and Clark and their party returning from their epic three-year journey deep into the North American continent. The explorers were saluted with artillery fire from the fort and Lewis and Clark were invited to spend the night in the Hunt house where a feather bed was prepared for them.

Apparently three years of roughing it had its effect on Lewis and Clark. As for the feather bed "they could not endure it," Hunt wrote. They instead laid out Buffalo robes and slept on the floor in their more accustomed frontier style.

A NIGHT IN THE SWAMP

In the summer of 1818 John Hunt accompanied his sister Mary on a journey from Cincinnati to Detroit. Near Defiance she was thrown from her horse and knocked senseless. She recovered somewhat and they made it to town where they spent the night.

The next night they stayed in a "log shantee" near what is now the hamlet of Hull Prairie in Wood County deep in the Great Black Swamp. Sharing their humble abode was a French trapper and hordes of mosquitoes.

"I thought the musquetos would devour my sister in spite of my efforts," Hunt recalled. He put his still-injured sister on his saddle in the corner of the shack, cut two tree branches, and "sat in front of her and kept both arms going until I became quite exhausted and what to do I did not know."

Around dark he heard the French trapper climb onto the roof of the structure and asked him what he was doing. "He said that when due fell it wet the musquetos wings so they could not reach the roof." Hunt heeded the advice, cut some long grass for a bed and got his sister up on the roof where they slept soundly the rest of the night. However when the sun rose "Mr. Musqueto tuned his pipes and came at us." Hunt and his sister eventually made it safely to Detroit.

MURDER AND REVENGE IN AN INDIAN VILLAGE

Hunt's memoirs tell the story of an Indian chief and his wife who lived on a tract of land called Blanchard Fork near what is now the city of Ottawa in Putnam County. He was fond of the couple and traded with them regularly.

They had a handsome son of whom they were quite proud and who at the age of 21 married a young squaw from the Indian village of Tontogany. After being married about four months, the son returned from a deer hunt and found his wife painting the face of a young chief and, in a fit of jealousy, killed him.

The friends of the young chief demanded a ransom of three horses to spare the life of the son, a payment his mother was most willing to make. The son however instructed his mother not to "give even a needle for his life," Hunt wrote. The son instead wanted to follow the Indian custom of sitting at the head of the corpse between sunrise and sunset the next day. If no one had confronted him by sunset he was cleared of his deed, according to custom.

He sat in a tent at the head of the corpse all day the next day and just as the sun was setting was approached by a friend of the man he had killed. The friend of his victim said to him "are you ready to pay or die," Hunt recalled. "His reply was not one needle will I give. He was dispatched at once being Stabed through his body he fell dead with hardly a struggle."

THE GREAT GATHERING OF 1817

In 1817, a call went out to all the Indian tribes of northwest Ohio and parts of northeast Indiana to gather in Maumee in September for the negotiating of the Treaty of 1817. The Treaty of Greenville (Ohio) in 1795 had left sizable tracts of land to tribes in these areas and this treaty was basically designed to take most of that away.

In the winter of that year Hunt and a partner had completed the building of a large two-story cabin in Maumee, an "elegant hued log Mansion" according to Hunt. It became such a popular stopping place for travelers that they decided to make it a frontier hotel and named it Bachellors Hall. It was to be the headquarters for the large American delegation coming to negotiate the treaty.

Around the first of September the Indian tribes began to congregate on the banks of the Maumee River. By the middle of the month, the Maumee Valley swelled with an estimated 8,000 Indians from 12 tribes. Their camps lined both sides of the river for miles. There were over 500 whites on hand for the occasion as well and virtually every square inch of Bachellors Hall was covered with a sleeping body at night.

The Shawnees and Senecas camped near Fort Meigs and "I must say I never saw so fine Indian dancing, and music made by these two tribes," Hunt wrote. The tribes "formed a ring of about three hundred Women around the fire around which drummers and singers were placed, and around the Women from five to seven hundred men would dance."

Some of the American delegates received special invitations to view the dancing and the sound of drums and Indian song echoed through the Maumee Valley late into the nights. With such a large number of Indians the treaty negotiations lasted several weeks. There was some protest—one Ottawa warrior told the American delegates that they would cheat the Indians until they had not enough land to build a fire on—and two tribes refused to sign the treaty. Negotiations were concluded on September 29th and the Americans gained control over land in northwest Ohio and parts of Indiana in exchange for about $100,000 in goods.

After the government treaty commissioners had departed, whiskey boats, which had stayed out of sight until then, moved in to sell whiskey to the Indians and a night of heavy drinking followed. The next morning the slope between Maumee city and the river "was filled with drunken Indians, Squaws, and children asleep with the Sun Shining in their faces and perspiration running off of them in great drops," Hunt wrote. "It took them one week to get over their drunken Spree..."

Hunt went on to note the devastating effect the loss of land and the white man's whiskey had on the area's Ottawa Indians saying that at the time of the treaty over 1,500 Ottawas lived on the Maumee, Blanchard, and Auglaize Rivers and their tributaries. "At this time (1871) they do not number more than one hundred and fifty."

A FEARSOME FELLOW

Of all the Indians Hunt knew, a Shawnee named Peshewton "was the worst, he was indeed a perfect devil." Hunt described him as a terror to his tribe who was married several times and who would kill his wives when he tired of them and mutilate their bodies.

Two cousins of one of the wives plotted to take their revenge while traveling with Peshewton from Wapakoneta to Fort Malden in Ontario. In the post War of 1812 years Indians frequently went to Fort Malden to receive goods from the British. The three stopped at a trading post near Monroe, Michigan to drink. There they planned to wait until Peshewton was drunk and attack him.

At the given moment one of the cousins struck Peshewton in the back with his tomahawk while the other began stabbing him. Despite being severely wounded, Peshewton managed to fight off and kill both his attackers and eventually recovered from his wounds.

Several months later Peshewton came to Hunt's Maumee store bragging about his deeds and borrowed ten dollars, leaving as collateral a blanket worth about $15. He told Hunt if he had not returned in a year to sell the blanket. Nearly three years passed with no Peshewton and Hunt went ahead and sold the blanket.

A few months later, the year was probably 1821, Peshewton walked in and demanded his blanket. Hunt explained that he had sold it as agreed but an angry Peshewton told him he would return in 10 days and wanted either the blanket or $20.

Peshewton returned as promised and he and a second Indian with tomahawks drawn stormed into the store and again demanded the money or the blanket. Hunt was alone as his clerks had gone to breakfast. But he had with him a rifle that had recently been found in the woods near the skeleton of a War of 1812 soldier. The gun was unloaded but had been cleaned and oiled and had its bayonet attached.

"I seized the Gun presenting the bayonet towards his breast across the counter replied to him that he was a damed raskeil and looking Streight in the eye Said go away or I will kill you," Hunt recalled. "He Supposed the gun loaded and much to my surprise and relief they put their tomahawks up and left the Store."

Peshewton and his partner went up the river to Waterville and to a trading post run by one Anthony Lapoint. There they demanded and got $20 from the frightened merchant, saying that what one white man owes another must pay.

Hunt encountered Peshewton several more times in the next couple of years, always casting a wary eye in his direction. Finally at Fort Malden a young chief named White Feather, a relative of one of the murdered wives, got the jump on Peshewton and stabbed him to death. "Thus perished one of the most cruel, heartless men in my opinion who ever lived," Hunt wrote. "It was a great relief not only to his own people but to other tribes living near him."

Chapter IV:

THE SPAFFORD BELL

In the Willard V. Way Library in Perrysburg is a glass display case inside of which hangs an old bell. Silent now, this bell could ring out rich historical tale, at least a version of one as told in a number of local history books.

The year was 1834 and the growing settlement of Perrysburg was proud of its fine hotel, the Exchange Hotel on West Front Street, built in 1823 by Jarvis Spafford. Spafford decided his hotel should have a bell with which to properly call his guests to dinner. He traveled to the nearest bell foundry, which was in Detroit, to have it cast. As the bellsmith ran a little short on metal, Spafford contributed 36 Spanish silver dollars into the melt. The bell was signed S. Davis, Detroit M.T. 1834, the M.T. standing for Michigan Territory as Michigan was not yet a state.

The innkeeper Spafford returned to Perrysburg with his prized bell and hung it in a tree adjacent to his hotel for all to admire. And many did admire it including the local population of Indians still living in the area. Fascinated with its sound, some of the Indians climbed the tree to ring it, causing guests to show up to meals prematurely. Things got worse when some of the Indians took to ringing the bell at night much to the exasperation of Spafford and his sleeping guests. It got to be routine for a bleary-eyed Spafford to drag himself out of bed in the wee hours to run off a group of bell-ringing Indians.

One morning Spafford arose to find his prized bell gone, stolen by a group of Indians. He formed a posse with two other men and set off in hot pursuit, following their trail for three days with no luck. The fourth morning they awoke at their camp near Upper Sandusky and, while enjoying a breakfast of venison and whiskey, heard a bell ringing in the distance.

After a ride through brush and high grass they came upon a clearing and, to their astonishment, there was the bell tied to the neck of a pony. One historical version says the pony was being driven in a circle by Indians who were delighting in its ringing while another version says the pony was grazing on grass with no Indians around.

The bell was retrieved and the trio rode back to Perrysburg, imbibing in a good deal of whiskey along the way. With his bell safely back, a wiser Spafford attached his bell to the hotel building in a heavy frame that prevented theft and unwanted nocturnal ringing.

The Exchange Hotel eventually went out of business and the bell traveled to Fort Wayne, then to Elmore, OH where it called guests to meals at the old Elmore House hotel. Over time it was brought back to Perrysburg and the library, a far more sedate setting than it had in its early years.

The Exchange Hotel building, going on two centuries old, still stands at 140 West Front Street. It now houses a dentist office. However the tree the Indians rang the bell from is long gone.

On the other hand, there was a letter sent to the editor of the *Perrysburg Journal* newspaper in 1890 by a man named George McNight and attested to by his friend, Henry Wygant, which disputes the above. "The plain facts concerning the bell I will give you," McNight wrote.

"Mr. Henry Wygant and I were boys when that bell was brought here from Detroit. It was unloaded from the stagecoach and was hung in a heavy iron frame. The next day Mr. Wygant's father and others assisted in placing the bell on the top of the hotel, and not in the tree as stated. The bell was never stolen."

Now this could be a case of the truth getting in the way of a good tale. However the accuracy of George McNight's childhood recollection will never be known; his letter was written 56 years after the alleged event. It's possible the version of events in his memory began after the bell was rescued from its kidnappers and the heavy frame was installed to prevent further theft. What is known is that there's always some degree of fiction sprinkled throughout the pages of recorded history.

The Spafford Bell, which allegedly went on a wild ride in 1834, now hangs quietly in the Willard V. Way Public Library, Perrysburg.

Chapter V:

THE WORST ROAD IN AMERICA

The route known as US 20 that runs between Perrysburg and Fremont is an easy 30-mile journey, a straight, flat road that courses through farmland and small towns. A drive on this unremarkable stretch today gives few clues to its past, that of a muck and mire-choked, tavern-lined "highway" that at one time had the reputation of being the worst in the country.

Known then as the Maumee and Western Reserve Road, the reason for the early difficulties of the route was simple. This road had as its bed the Great Black Swamp.

The roadway had its beginnings in an 1808 treaty that stipulated that a strip of land 120 feet wide running from Fremont, then called Lower Sandusky, to the Maumee River be used as a public highway. It was surveyed in 1811 but little in the way of any improvements were made and it remained an arduous crawl through swamp and stands of towering trees, some 120 feet tall. However it served as a guide through a hostile terrain and, as settlers streamed westward, many used it as there was simply no alternative.

One historical account lamented "it would be difficult to describe this worst of all roads and the agony bordering on despair to which the emigrant was reduced in his effort to pass over to the land flowing with milk and honey beyond."

Stories of people abandoning hopelessly mired wagons and carriages, baggage and all, were not uncommon. In addition to the challenges of the terrain, the usual Great Black Swamp plagues of floods in the spring, hordes of mosquitoes in summer, and swamp fever in the fall were present.

In 1823 Congress authorized more work on the road and by 1827 the great trees that stood in its path had been felled and some rudimentary drainage ditches had been dug. Still it remained a series of wagon-sucking mud holes most of the year save for in the height of a dry summer or the frozen grip of a cold winter.

The mud along the route proved to be of epic proportions and the more the route was used the more of a quagmire it became. Attempts to fill the holes with more dirt made the problem worse by simply creating more mud. When horse-drawn wagons and carriages traveling the route "arrived at either end of the line, the cart, the driver, and the horses often presented an almost indistinguishable mass of slowly moving mud," according to an historical description.

With the number of travelers increasing, the 1820's and early 1830's saw numerous taverns sprout along the route. By 1834 there were 31 taverns between Fremont and Perrysburg, or an average of a tavern every mile. These taverns frequently were little more than rough, log cabins, especially the ones located between towns.

But the proprietors of these taverns provided three essential services; food, lodging, and most importantly, teams of strong oxen to pull wagons out of the mud. Small fortunes were made by providing these services.

It was not unusual for a traveling party to stay at the same tavern two or three nights just getting through a particularly bad stretch of terrain. Indeed, the sheer number of taverns present in such a short length of road gives an idea of how painfully slow a traveler's progress could be.

Those in the mud-hauling business divided up the road among themselves, at times selling the rights to their particular mud hole when they tired of it. One pioneer heading for Michigan spent his life savings of $100 paying to get pulled through the mud. So he set up on his own mud hole, made his money back, and continued on.

There were, of course, some unscrupulous tavern operators

who overcharged for their services. But their presence as a whole on the route provided a refuge for tired travelers who had likely spent a good part of their day cursing up a storm over mired horses and wagons. At the taverns they could unwind, dry out by a warm fire, drink some whiskey and catch up on the news of the day.

The notorious reputation of the Maumee and Western Reserve Road eventually brought it the attention it deserved. In 1838 after years of hearing bitter complaints the state of Ohio authorized money for it to be paved with broken stone, a process known as macadamizing, with tolls to be charged to recover the costs. Drainage ditches and culverts were also dug and limestone mile markers, many which still stand, were erected.

A journal entry of a woman traveling the road on her way to Wisconsin in 1846 gives an idea of how much it changed in ten years "Now we found a good road, a high turnpike paved with broken stone, but we had to pay an 81 cent toll." The Maumee and Western Reserve Road had gone from being perhaps the worst in America to being one of the best.

Old, stone mile markers still stand along US 20 between Fremont and Perrysburg, once the Maumee and Western Reserve Road. From the above marker it is 9 miles to Lower Sandusky, now Fremont, and 22 miles to Perrysburg.

Chapter VI:

THE COMPASSIONATE WARRIOR

The site now is a just a rolling, grassy bluff high above the Maumee River. Only the mounds of earth and a faded historical marker serve as reminders of the fort that once stood there.

For once in the now sedate 1900 block of River Road in Maumee stood Fort Miamis, a British fort built in 1794 and used again by them during the War of 1812. It was during the latter that a drama of cowardice and courage, savagery and sympathy, was played out on a warm May day in 1813. The central player in this was the great Shawnee Chief Tecumseh.

Tecumseh was a remarkable person; a warrior, visionary, and orator who had spent his life futilely resisting the tide of white encroachment on Indian lands in the Ohio and Indiana areas. Born around 1768 near what is now Piqua, Ohio, he frequently traveled through the Maumee River Valley and northwest Ohio. As a young brave he fought against the Americans and General "Mad Anthony" Wayne at the Battle of Fallen Timbers in 1794.

Following that defeat, he refused to acknowledge the Treaty of Greenville in 1795 that ceded most of the Ohio lands to the whites and continued to organize tribes from the Midwest and South to resist the tide of white settlement. His stature rose in Indian society and he became well-known and highly respected among his peers, a leader whose speeches held audiences spellbound. Along the way he also developed a distaste for the torture and abuse of prisoners that was a common practice among many tribes.

Tecumseh and his Indian allies did enjoy some military success in the early 1800's. Then came the defeat of his brother's forces at the Battle of Tippecanoe in Indiana in 1811 which appeared to mean the collapse of Indian military resistance in this region.

However in 1812 war erupted again between the United States and England and the British promised land if Tecumseh and his confederation fought with them. The Shawnee chief knew this would be his best and last chance. He and his army joined the British at Fort Malden in Amherstburg, Ontario where the Detroit River flows into Lake Erie. With the British, Tecumseh was accorded the status of a brigadier general.

In the spring of 1813 an American army, led by General William Henry Harrison, completed the building of Fort Meigs on the bluffs of the Maumee River in what is now Perrysburg. On May 1st the British and a Tecumseh-led Indian force began a siege of Fort Meigs. As the Americans stayed put inside the fort, the event was primarily an exchange of cannon fire with little face-to-face fighting.

Then on May 5th a detachment of Kentucky soldiers marching down the Maumee River to join Harrison were ordered to first spike British cannons across the river and return to the fort immediately afterward before a counterattack could be mounted. Their mission completed, the eager soldiers fell for an Indian ruse and chased some of them into the woods where they were soon surrounded. In the debacle that followed, only 150 of the original 800 Kentuckians made it back to Fort Meigs, the rest being killed or captured.

The captives were led downriver to old Fort Miamis where an ugly scene unfolded. Some of the Indians began attacking the prisoners, killing and scalping many. The British stood idly by making only token attempts to stop the slaughter. Screams of agony and terror mingled with the thud of tomahawks slamming into human flesh and bone.

When Tecumseh, who had remained near the cannons, heard of the slaughter taking place he seized a horse and raced toward Fort Miamis. What happened next was later recounted by British and American soldiers and by a British Indian agent familiar with the Shawnee tongue.

Tecumseh thundered through the gates of the fort and, upon seeing 40 or more dead Kentuckians, exploded in anger. He leaped from his horse, threw one Indian to the ground, drew his knife, and threatened to kill the next one who harmed another soldier.

A stunned silence settled over the fort. Then Tecumseh, with a look of great despair on his face, glanced toward the sky with tears in his eyes and said "Oh what will become of my Indians?"

He then turned his attention to the British commanders and demanded to know why they hadn't stopped the slaughter. "Sir, your Indians cannot be commanded," the British general in charge replied.

"Begone!," Tecumseh shouted back. "You are unfit to command. Go and put on petticoats." Afterward, no more Americans were harmed.

Tecumseh's despair that day would soon prove to be prophetic. The May siege of Fort Meigs and a similar one in late July were basically failures. Many of the Indians fighting with Tecumseh grew disillusioned and returned to their tribes.

Tecumseh and his remaining Indians withdrew with the British to Amherstburg and Fort Malden. On September 10th a British naval fleet from Amherstburg was defeated in the Battle of Lake Erie and soon after Harrison and his army marched from Fort Meigs to attack Fort Malden.

The British made plans to burn the fort and retreat inland where they hoped to gain some strategic advantage over the larger American force. Before they did, however, Tecumseh gave his final recorded speech to a crowd in Amherstburg on September 19, 1813. "Our lives are in the hands of the Great Spirit," he told the gathering in closing, "we are determined to defend our lands and if it is His will, we wish to leave our bones upon them."

On October 5th, under a blue sky cast with the crimson and gold colors of autumn, the American army caught up with the British and Indians near the Thames River about 50 miles north of Amherstburg. There a brief battle turned into a rout and

Tecumseh was shot dead, leaving his bones upon the land just as he had prophesied. Dying with him were any remaining dreams of Indian homelands east of the Mississippi River.

No one will ever know how much more blood would have soaked the ground at Fort Miamis that May day without Tecumseh's intercession. The number of Kentucky soldiers who lived to see their farms and families again who might otherwise have been killed will also never be known.

What is known is that Tecumseh, the remarkable warrior, orator, and leader, cast his shadow throughout northwest Ohio and the Great Black Swamp. A shadow, perhaps, as large as any cast there.

Chapter VII:

SOLDIER OF THE AMERICAN REVOLUTION

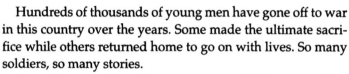

Hundreds of thousands of young men have gone off to war in this country over the years. Some made the ultimate sacrifice while others returned home to go on with lives. So many soldiers, so many stories.

One of those soldiers lies at rest atop a hill just east of the village of Bradner on the Wood-Sandusky county line. His name is Abraham William McBurney, veteran of the American Revolution. His marble marker faces west, painted with a soft glow by thousands of sunsets over time. His story, like those of so many who fought in that long ago war, has too few pages.

What little local history does tell us is that he left his homeland of Ireland in 1775 and came to America to join the 13 colonies fight to throw off their British rulers. He served through the end of the war and came westward to the Ohio wilderness with General "Mad Anthony" Wayne. He fought in the Ohio Indian Wars in the 1790's, which culminated with the Battle of Fallen Timbers in August, 1794 on the Maumee River, and remained. In 1835 when well into his seventies he came to a rise in Wood County called Mt. Prospect in the heart of the Great Black Swamp, an isolated frontier outpost that was the early beginnings of Bradner. It was there he lived his final days, one of the handful of veterans of the Revolutionary War to have migrated this far West.

He died in 1837 and was buried at the highest point in Mt. Prospect, now Chestnut Grove Cemetery, the first white person to be buried there. He never married and he left no relatives or known written record. His story, gathered from the fading memories of aging 19th century settlers, goes no further. There must be more.

Over 60 years passed between the time an adventure-seeking Irish lad made the bounding ocean voyage from the Old World to the New and a tired old man breathed his last, in a rugged cabin in a lonely place. In those six decades McBurney was a soldier in two military campaigns, both crucibles in which was fired the geo-political destiny of the United States; the overthrow of British rule and the opening of the Northwest Territory to white settlement.

In those six decades he moved restlessly west in apparent preference for the untamed and unordered ways of frontier life. In those six decades he must have witnessed countless scenes now embroidered on the fabric of American history. And in those six decades, he left few footprints.

Perhaps he served under Anthony Wayne in the Revolution and, when Wayne was called out of retirement by President George Washington to raise an army and fight in the Ohio lands, he followed. He could have been enchanted by the Maumee River valley once his eyes fell upon it and decided to stay.

Historical observer Charles Evers of Bowling Green wrote in 1852, "Soldiers who came with Mad Anthony to the Maumee country never afterward tired of extolling its beauties, its fertilities, its fine forests of oak, walnut, poplar and other valuable timber-its rivers swarming with the lovely muscalunge and sturgeon, its myriads of 'red horse' (suckers), the gamey black bass and the fat, lubberly cat fish of such enormous proportions that a single fish made a meal for one of Wayne's cavalry companies at Defiance."

So starting about 1795 McBurney apparently lived in the Maumee Valley, one of the lone frontier hunters thought to be in the area at the time, enjoying its bounty, its beauty and its isolation. He must have witnessed some of the events of the spring and summer of 1813 when the Maumee Valley bristled with British and American soldiers and Indian warriors clashing in the War of 1812.

He also must have witnessed the slow trickle of settlers coming to the valley after the war, a movement substantially slowed by the barriers and challenges posed by the Great Black Swamp. He too must have walked the dusty streets of Perrysburg, laid out in 1816, and Maumee, established a year later.

In 1830 the federal government conducted its first census of the region and only 1100 people lived in all of Wood County. That number included all of what became Lucas County which was not organized until 1835. In that census, McBurney's name does not appear in the rolls of Wood or any of the surrounding counties.

Perhaps he lived well out of sight deep in the woods. Perhaps he was off hunting on the day the census taker stopped by his cabin. Or perhaps he smiled when he heard the census taker's questions and turned and walked away, thus guarding the anonymity his lifestyle suggests he preferred.

In the early 1830's settlers began to arrive in large numbers to the Maumee Valley and maybe this was just too much congestion for Abraham McBurney. In 1835 this old man who had seen so much in his three quarters of a century of living, limped into the inhospitable Great Black Swamp to Mt. Prospect to spend the last two years of his life. Maybe he knew someone there who would take in an old soldier in the sunset of his days.

He died on an unknown date in 1837. His grave lays next to the resting place of Phillip Hathaway who also came to Mt. Prospect in 1835 and fought in the War of 1812. Did these two veterans come to Mt. Prospect together? Did they swap tales of their respective wars against the King of England? Did Phillip Hathaway help carry Abraham McBurney to his grave, shovel some dirt, and linger for a few final thoughts and prayers for a fellow soldier? Like so many other questions about the life of this Revolutionary War veteran, the mists of time shroud the answers.

McBurney's grave lay unadorned for nearly a century until the Jane Washington Chapter of the Daughters of the American Revolution from Fostoria procured a marble marker with a bronze tablet. They dedicated the stone on Memorial Day, 1925 in a solemn ceremony, the last entry in a story whose pages are too few.

His marker looks down on Great Black Swamp lands he defied as an old man, just as he defied the expanse of the Atlantic Ocean as a young man leaving behind home and country to join a burgeoning young nation and its war with England. The tablet on his stone says simply "A. McBurney, Cont'l Army, Rev. War," its brevity a metaphor for the story of his life.

Grave of Revolutionary War veteran Abraham McBurney

in the Chestnut Grove Cemetery near Bradner, Ohio

Chapter VIII:

WOMEN OF THE MAUMEE VALLEY

History has been criticized by some as "his story," that is, the story of the experiences of men written by men with the roles and realities of women mentioned only here and there. The written history of the Great Black Swamp and Maumee Valley in the 19th century is no different, with emphasis on life as experienced by the man reflecting the social customs and structure of the time.

However in 1895 the Maumee Valley Pioneer Association did gather stories of some of the first women to come to northwest Ohio in a collection titled *Woman's Part in Pioneer Life*. Most of them were posthumous testimonials written by a daughter or son and tend to read similarly; "she was a woman of grace with good Christian morals," etc. However they do also provide a glimpse, albeit small, of what it was like for women living at what was then the edge of the world as they knew it.

MARY HUNT

Mary Hunt, wife of John Hunt of Maumee chronicled earlier, married John in Detroit in May, 1822. Her honeymoon was a three-day horseback ride to Maumee, arriving in a driving rain. Despite the frontier setting she loved the scenery of the Maumee Valley and her log home. "Here her kitchen was in the basement, dining room on the floor above (every meal being carried upstairs as there were then no 'dumb waiters'); and her bedroom in the upper story; an arrangement modern housekeepers would hardly call convenient or labor-saving."

Hunt was one who liked to stay busy. "But true it is that the busiest ones find the most time to help others, and, Mrs. Hunt, always watchful for the opportunity to do good, it was no unusual thing for her to bring home someone convalescing from bilious fever (so prevalent then on the Maumee) and care for her till strength returned... Here, for 30 years, her home was a center of hospitality to rich and poor alike."

Mary Hunt lived to the age of 81, dying in 1876 on Christmas morning in her Toledo home.

Mary Ralph Spafford

The story of Mary Ralph Spafford spreads over four and one-half pages. However in a good example of "his story" the first three pages are devoted to telling the story of her husband, Major Amos Spafford, generally credited for being the first settler in what became Perrysburg.

Spafford was a strong woman who bore six children and outlived all but one of them. She also was blessed with a good set of teeth that she kept through her 88 years, as her story points out. "She had a remarkable set of teeth, sufficient to masticate her food well up to the day of her death. [She] never complained of toothache, that dreadful affection. From childhood she made it a point to clean her teeth after eating."

While the above may seem an odd or frivolous thing to write about a person in this age of dental care, for someone to keep their teeth in a time when it was typical for age to lead to toothless smiles was no small feat.

Sally Wakeman Scott

Sally Wakeman Scott was born to a wealthy family in Connecticut in 1797. She came to the Maumee Valley in 1833 with her husband Jessup, the Toledo editor and civic leader of 19th century renown. An educated woman with a passion for music, her prized possession in her hinterland cabin was a piano she played for visitors.

The transition from educated East Coast society to frontier life was not an easy one for her or her husband but she "bore all the small privations and annoyances of life in the primitive town with high cheerfulness—always elated by prosperity and less depressed by adversity than he."

"Mud was the horror those days...The clay soil of Maumee and Perrysburg is almost unequaled in the world in sticky quality. The boys, when they returned from school or play in wet weather were literally plastered from toes to hips...The boys and mens pants when 'stood up' to dry around the open fires would sometime stand alone without legs in them and when dried or baked would require muscle and patience to beat them so as to bring the original cloth into sight and pliancy...Those were the things that tried women's souls."

Scott's optimism and positive outlook on life was tested plenty during her first ten years on the frontier. "When reverses came to my father's fortune and we lived at Miami (Maumee) growing poorer every year from 1838 to 1843 and my mother having to turn and twist the boys clothes to make them do and to put patches two or three deep, her unfailing cheerfulness was a staff and strength that my father greatly needed."

EMILY UNDERWOOD BALLOU

Emily Underwood was born on Independence Day in 1809 in New York and as a girl of nine journeyed across Lake Erie with her family on the *Walk-in-the-Water*, the first steamboat on the Great Lakes. The Underwoods arrived in September, 1818 in what is now Toledo where there were only "two rough houses built, both being of logs, one hewn and the other rough."

From there Emily, her parents, and seven siblings continued to Maumee to spend the winter with plans to settle in Indiana the following year. However death would cut a swath through the family. In a ten-week period beginning August 7, 1819, the ten-year-old girl watched three brothers and one sister be laid to rest, probably victims of ague or swamp fever, which was at its worst in late summer and fall. A year later she lost her mother. Emily, her father, and three remaining siblings settled in Maumee.

Emily married Orson Ballou in 1831 and in 1833 settled four miles west of Waterville in what was then wilderness. Her husband, who ran the grist mill in town, was gone much of the time. "Here for six years with a small clearing and proportionate cabin lived my mother, the nearest neighbor three miles away by trail," her son wrote.

On one occasion while chasing a groundhog for supper she started a small fire to smoke him out of his hole. What resulted was "a conflagration beyond her most sanguine expectations or wishes. The whole hill burned except where the cabin stood...she never knew what became of the groundhog."

Indians were regular visitors to the cabin and Emily Underwood Ballou enjoyed good relations with them, frequently trading her corn meal for the berries they gathered. "Always showing sympathy and kindness to the Indian, she was generally beloved and respected by them and, had there been a general uprising, there is no question she would have been unmolested."

SALLIE WIGHTMAN WILKINSON

Sallie Wightman Wilkinson came to the Maumee Valley in 1811 with her husband and three young children, and settled on the river beneath where Fort Meigs is today. The following summer she watched General William Hull and his American army march by on their way to Detroit as the War of 1812 was about to throw frontier life into chaos.

Weeks later when Hull surrendered Detroit without a fight, the Wilkinson family, along with their neighbors, fled in panic to Cleveland. They traveled Lake Erie in a crowded open boat, a blanket for a sail, keeping a good distance from shore beyond the range of rifle shot. In Sallie's bosom were six silver spoons, all she could save from her home.

Peace eventually returned to the Maumee and so did Sallie and her family in 1816 to the task of rebuilding their destroyed home. Their new cabin with two large rooms had a wooden floor made of ash, unusual in pioneer days, and a source of pride to her. Every week she had her sons scrub it with sand and water while her oldest daughter polished it with a piece of heavy linen cloth. In between it was swept with brooms bought from the Indians.

Wightman's religious roots ran deep on her family's side. She was a descendant of the last Christian martyr burned at the stake in England and could count a long family line of ministers who emigrated to New England seeking religious freedom. So it was natural that her large home served as a gathering place for religious services, the strains of hymns floating from it on Sunday mornings.

Her faith did not spare her from the heartbreak so prevalent in pioneer life. Of her five sons, only one lived beyond early adulthood. She died in 1839 at the age of 55.

Chapter IX:

THE TOLEDO WAR

When the universities of Ohio State and Michigan wage their annual gridiron grudge match around Thanksgiving every year, it marks a rivalry that dates back to 1835. For that was the year when men and their muskets from the Buckeye and Wolverine states lined up ready to fight it out in the so-called "Toledo War."

A boundary dispute had brewed up between the two states in the early 1800's over the exact location of the state line. In short, Michigan's version would have placed all of what is now Toledo in that state, a literal interpretation of the Northwest Ordinance of 1787, while Ohio claimed a proviso inserted in its application to Congress for statehood in 1803 allowed them some flexibility in the matter.

In the end, both sides believed the maps they wanted to believe and the controversy simmered on and off for decades. It came to a head in the 1830's when Congress insisted Michigan resolve its border dispute with Ohio prior to admission to the Union as a state. In the spring of 1834 Congress denied statehood to Michigan, a slap in the face, with one Ohio congressman suggesting that discussing the whole matter was a waste of time with Michigan being a "third or fourth rate power" and one hardly worthy of statehood.

Now anger was rising in the Wolverine state and, with an aggressive young territorial governor named Stevens Mason who was zealous on the issue of statehood, the boundary fight was on. Mix in on the part of both sides greed and, the mother of conflicts throughout time immemorial, politics, and the fight over the "Toledo Strip" quickly grew.

While there were side issues and agendas too numerous to list associated with the dispute, there was one overriding belief which created such interest over the territory. It was the prospect that Toledo would become the commanding economic and industrial center of the Great Lakes, a crown later placed on the head of Chicago as the country continued to bulge westward.

In early 1835 the Ohio legislature passed a law that extended its jurisdiction over the area. Michigan immediately responded with the Pains and Penalties Act which criminalized such action to the tune of a $1,000 fine and/or five years hard labor. Ohio upped the ante when Governor Robert Lucas announced he was sending three commissioners to the disputed area in April to rerun the state line in Ohio's favor, a move that sent Michigan Governor Mason into a rage. Clearly, cooler heads were not prevailing.

Both sides appealed to Washington and President Andrew Jackson who appointed a commission to arbitrate the dispute. Both governors were fellow Democrats and Jackson did not want to alienate either one. However Ohio proceeded with its plans to rerun the state line.

In late March, 1835 Ohio Governor Lucas and his party of surveyors left for Perrysburg and the excited frontier town awaited his arrival. He arrived there April 2nd to the shouts of the crowd, the firing of cannons, and the pealing of bells. Actually there had been several unplanned rehearsals of the greeting as no one was sure what the governor looked like and other travelers arriving in town had been mistaken for the governor's party, strangers astonished by such a welcome.

Events now began to converge. On April 3rd the arbitrators from Washington arrived in Toledo. On April 4th Michigan held elections to select delegates to a constitutional convention for the purpose of achieving statehood. On April 5th one of the Washington arbitrators wrote to President Jackson of the fierce determination of Ohio Governor Lucas to get his way.

This was confirmed when Lucas held an election of township officers in the disputed territory the next day, an event that caused Michigan to enforce the Pains and Penalties Act.

On April 8th the Monroe County sheriff arrived in Toledo with a posse and forcibly entered the home of well-known Toledo pioneer Major Benjamin Stickney who was out of town and arrested two of his guests, roughing up other members of the household in the process. The two guests were bound and hauled off to Monroe where they were released on bail two days later.

When the colorful Stickney learned of the event he minced no words in describing the incident in the *Toledo Gazette*, a version later carried in Washington D.C.'s *National Intelligencer*. He decried Michigan's "band of ruffians" and their "monstrous violence" and "inhuman malignity." He predicted that both sides were heading toward "a horrid Border War" and concluded that Ohioans would turn out en masse "and restrain the savage barbarity of the hordes of the north."

On April 10th the Washington arbitrators, now in Monroe, in a letter to President Jackson described the situation there as "men galloping about—guns getting ready—wagons being filled with people and hurrying off, and everybody in commotion." On April 11th around two hundred armed Michiganders marched to Toledo. With no opposing Ohio force to confront them they marched through the streets of Toledo engaging in petty mischief and tying the state flag of Ohio to the tail of a horse and dragging it through the mud before returning north.

Two weeks later, matters came to a head in a confrontation that came to be known as the Battle of Phillips Corner. On April 26th an Ohio surveying party and its guards, while resting on the Sabbath, were set upon by the Lenawee County sheriff and a posse of 30 armed men as they camped in a field in what is now Fulton County in Ohio. Most of the group fled headlong back toward Perrysburg. But nine of the guards took refuge in a small cabin where they were quickly surrounded.

After a delay they agreed to leave the cabin and surrender, but upon emerging attempted a run for the woods. The Michigan posse opened fire, sending a volley of bullets over the heads of the fleeing Buckeye State soldiers who quickly came to their senses and surrendered. The only casualty was a shirt ripped by a musket ball. They were marched to Tecumseh, Michigan where most of them posted bail or were released, save for one who refused to post bail on general principle.

After this, hostilities in the field quieted a bit and the war shifted back to the halls of government. In a special legislative session in June, Ohio passed a law calling for three to seven years hard labor for any one committing the "forcible abduction of citizens of Ohio." In addition, legislation was passed establishing a county in the disputed area to be named Lucas County after the governor, and for a Common Pleas Court session to be held there the first Monday in September to make the whole thing official. In the meantime, three Ohio delegates were to go to Washington to appeal the state's case directly to President Jackson.

Even though Ohio's case was legally weaker than Michigan's, the Ohio delegates in Washington barely worked up a sweat. Upon meeting with President Jackson they were told in so many words "write down what you want and give it to me." What the delegates came away with was that Michigan should cease enforcement and prosecutions under the Pains and Penalties Act, that Ohio could continue its resurvey of the state line, and that persons living in the disputed territory could follow the laws of the state they preferred until Congress decided the whole jurisdiction matter on a permanent basis the following year, a decision that would very likely be in Ohio's favor.

President Jackson was no fool. For Ohio was a state and Michigan was not. Ohio had voting senators and representatives and Michigan did not. And, most importantly, Ohio had voting presidential electors, Michigan did not, and Jackson wanted his vice-president and close friend Martin Van Buren to succeed him as president the following year.

However Michigan Governor Mason ignored the directive from Washington and hostilities continued in the Toledo Strip in the spring and early summer of 1835. During this time both sides engaged in raising citizen militias, ragtag armies armed with everything from muskets to pitchforks to broomsticks.

The armies would train and march and were known for drinking, bragging, and "appropriating" pigs and chickens from local citizens along the away as much as anything else.

In mid-July the Monroe County sheriff attempted to arrest Two Stickney, the son of Benjamin Stickney (his other son was named One), who responded by stabbing a deputy in the arm and fleeing to Columbus. On July 17th a mob of 250 armed Wolverine warriors led by the Monroe County sheriff came to Toledo to arrest the offender and sacked the offices of the *Toledo Gazette* newspaper. As Two Stickney was long gone they arrested old Benjamin himself who, kicking and screaming, had to have his legs tied together under the horse for transportation back to Monroe. There he spent time in the Monroe jail "peeping through the grates of a loathsome prison for the monstrous crime of having acted as judge of an election within the state of Ohio," as he later put it.

There was to be one more major confrontation in the Toledo War. And that would revolve around the determination of Ohio to hold a Common Pleas Court session to make official appointments in its newly created county of Lucas the first Monday in September, and the equal determination of Michigan to stop it. Both sides assembled militias in preparation for the event and the potential for genuine bloodshed was real. However when the Ohio people learned that the Michigan army would be quite a bit larger than their own, they resorted to strategy.

As the September 7th date drew near the Michigan army assembled north of Toledo ready to ride into town in the morning to break up the court session and arrest the Ohio officials. However in the wee hours, Ohio officials crept into town from Perrysburg and opened a court session in an old schoolhouse at 3:00 a.m. In a nervous 15 or 20 minute session, candlelight proceedings were conducted and appointments were made, the minutes of which were deposited in the crown of the high hat of the court clerk. Court was adjourned and the party retired to a hotel at Summit and Elm streets for a celebratory drink.

While toasting their success a prankster ran in saying the Michigan army was on its way and the group bolted from the

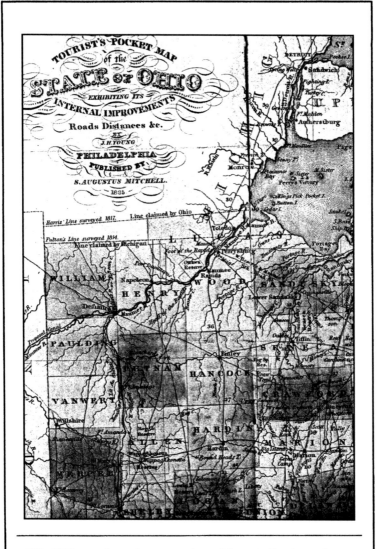

This 1835 map shows the two versions of the state line in northwest Ohio. The southern line claimed by Michigan would have put all of Toledo in the Wolverine state. (The Tourist's Pocket Map of the State of Ohio, courtesy of the Ward M. Canaday Center for Special Collections, University of Toledo Libraries.)

bar leaving spilled glasses and an unpaid tab in their wake. In a mad, horseback dash down the Maumee River, the hat of the clerk containing the minutes was knocked off by a tree branch. However the papers were later retrieved, thus the first official business of Lucas County was recorded.

The next morning the Michigan army rode in ready for a fight, but there was no fight to be had. After milling around for a couple of days drinking and insulting and engaging in petty theft from local citizens, the bored ragtag army returned to their Michigan homes. When Michigan officials learned of Ohio's deception, all they could do is bluster helplessly. After that most of the starch went out of the Toledo War.

In the following months Washington made it clear that in order to attain its desired statehood, Michigan must give up the Toledo Strip. As compensation the Wolverine state would receive the Upper Peninsula, then regarded as a howling wilderness and an area scoffed at by one Detroit newspaper as "the region of perpetual snows." Eventually Michigan agreed and in January, 1837 it became the nation's newest state.

No one died in the Toledo War. A deputy was stabbed in the arm, people were roughed up and thrown in jail, pigs and chickens were stolen, politicians postured and pontificated, and pride and egos on both sides were gored.

In the end Ohio got exactly what it wanted while Michigan was forced to compromise. But in the Upper Peninsula, Michigan gained thousands of square miles of territory rich in minerals and timber and one that is a popular recreational area today. Bitterness between the two states soon faded, feelings now resurrected once a year on a football field in late November.

Chapter X:

COLONEL DRESDEN HOWARD

Near the rural and quiet center of Fulton County, a road slopes from flat farmland to a sun-dappled valley in a hamlet called Winameg. The silence of the valley there is broken only by the whispering waters of Bad Creek and the sound of an occasional passing auto. A couple of historical markers give a peek into this serene setting's past, telling of two men and a tree that once cast shadows there; Colonel Dresden Howard, his friend Chief Winameg, and a tree known as the Council Oak.

Howard was a government interpreter who came to the valley as a youth and met Chief Winameg, the leader of a Potawatomie Indian band living there whose hair had been "whitened by the snows of a hundred winters." It was a time when the sun was rising on the white man's world and setting fast on the world of the Indian. From the valley floor rose a mighty oak tree, the Council Oak. Under its spreading boughs on the valley floor the old chief would sit with his young friend, temporary shelter from a world closing in.

During Dresden Howard's lifetime he witnessed a northwest Ohio that went from having a large number of Indians living in it to one that had virtually none. When he was an older man he wrote down some of his thoughts and recollections of that era, perspectives unique as his friendship with and concern for the Indians contrasted sharply with the prevailing attitudes of his time and his people.

Howard was born in New York in 1817 and came to Grand Rapids, Ohio with his family in 1821. His father was a fur trader and established a number of trading posts in the area. He spent his boyhood days in the 1820's with Indian playmates in a large Ottawa village that still existed across the river from Grand Rapids. He also attended school with them at the Presbyterian Mission School north of town. The last Indian military resistance in the area had been crushed in the War of 1812 and white settlers were now coming to the region.

By the time he was a teenager, Howard was fluent in five Indian languages and was welcome at any Native campfire. In the 1830's government pressure to exile the Indians to the West became intense, and Howard, at the early age of 15, became a government interpreter in talks between the two groups. The Indians trusted Howard as his familiarity with their language and ways assured better communication. In addition, he would not deceive them as some white interpreters had.

Howard, who was given the title of colonel as was the custom for interpreters in those days, went about his duties with a heavy heart. While he personally disliked the policy of Indian removal he knew for them to stay would surely mean a slow death as there simply would be no allowance for them in the white man's world. The land they had lived on for centuries was being surveyed and sold out from under them to the settlers flocking to the region. At least in the open lands beyond the Mississippi River they would have a chance, albeit small, at surviving as a people.

One of the trading posts established by Howard's father was in the Potawatomie camp of Chief Winameg, a once thriving Indian village on the banks of Bad Creek. The spiritual center of the village was the Council Oak, a white oak on the north side of the creek dating to the 1600's whose trunk was nearly six feet in diameter.

The Council Oak had heard many things over the years. The murmur of conversation and the crackle of council fires rose through its branches during Indian councils. The sounds of laughter and shouts of joy echoed about it during tribal feasts and celebrations. And much darker sounds radiated from under its shade during warring years as Indian prisoners, lashed to an upside down impression of a man carved into its bark, met a gruesome fate.

In the 1830's the tree heard a saddened, old chief who had seen so much in his century of living tell an attentive young listener of the days gone by, days that would never return. He told Howard of a time when a great Potawatomie village lined the valley with hundreds of tribal lodges, when the woods were rich in game, the rivers abundant with fish and beaver, and the fields filled with corn, squash, beans, and pumpkins. It was a time when his people were numerous, secure, and happy.

"There was at times such an air of despondancy in the old man's voice and I could discern the pain he felt when recounting the happy scenes of his people when all was theirs as far as the eye could reach," Howard wrote. "Now the pale face has taken all; the spot of his council fires, the graves of his dead, and the little spot upon which he pitched his tent was not his."

During the 1830's Howard participated in a number of negotiations between the government and Indians. He traveled west with one group of Ottawas and Potawatomies, staying with them to Fort Leavenworth in Kansas assuring they passed safely through hostile, white settlements. By 1840 virtually all Indians were gone from northwest Ohio, save for scattered families and groups.

In 1842 Howard built a fine home on the north side of the valley, a four-pillared, colonial mansion that still stands, and established a farm. Chief Winameg, who did not go west, continued to eke out a living in the area for a time until his death. As was his wish he was buried near the shadow of the Council Oak in the valley he loved so much.

The years were good to Dresden Howard and his farm on the grounds of the old Potawatomie village was a prosperous one. The new village that sprang up around it was named Winameg in honor of the old chief. In Howard's waning years he would wander about his farm, at times passing through the orchard, site of an old tribal burying ground. There, visages of the past would haunt him.

"Often in walking through the orchard, images of these departed braves rise before me, and I see them in all their paint and savage dress appearing to reproach me for occupying and trampling upon the graves of their departed heroes and the dead ashes of their extinguished council fires. And, as I am about to reply that I am still their friend and will care, while I live, for the graves of their dead warriors the illusion disappears and the inmates of those graves are as silent as they have been for half a century..."

Howard always regretted the manner in which his race dealt with the Indians. In one of his writings he lamented, "I may be censured for my sympathy for these poor wandering people driven from place to place and finally exterminated but I still say better to have given them homes and made friends of them than to have robbed and starved and made enemies of them as we did."

Dresden Howard became influential in the development of Fulton County and served in a number of posts, including that of state senator, before he died at the age of 80 in 1897. Before his death he selected a spot to be buried at the foot of the hill below his home under the shade of the Council Oak near his friend Chief Winameg. Next to him rests his wife Mary who lived until 1915. At his funeral he was eulogized as "one of God's noblemen and one who made the world better for having lived in it."

The Council Oak would live another hundred years before the ravages of time and disease brought about its demise in 1992. In its over three hundred years of living, the land around it underwent a dramatic physical and cultural transformation. While the tree no longer stands, the stump of its great trunk remains. Over time it too will rejoin the earth along with the two friends that once sat beneath its branches.

Colonel Dresden Howard as he appeared later in life. (Photo courtesy of Fulton County Historical Society, Wauseon).

The Council Oak as it appeared in the early 1950's. The tree died of disease and was cut down in 1992, its age estimated at 300 years. (Photo courtesy of Fulton County Historical Society).

Chapter XI:

WOOD COUNTY TALES

Charles Evers was born in Wood County in Miltonville in 1837, a Maumee River town that long ago slipped into the pages of history. He attended Oberlin College until the Civil War broke out and joined the Union army and served three years before being shot in the leg and taken prisoner. He spent three starving months in a Confederate POW camp before being paroled just in time for surgeons to save his badly injured leg.

Evers came home disabled and was elected Wood County sheriff in 1864. He later became part owner of the *Wood County Sentinel* newspaper and took an interest in the writing of the history of the area. He died in July, 1909, and later that year his daughter published *Pioneer Scrapbook*, a book of historical tales, mostly of Wood County, from which the following four stories were drawn.

A CHILD LOST

One of the many problems frontier parents had to cope with was having a child wander away from their cabin and get lost in the woods. In the fall of 1835 in Bloom Township in southern Wood County a five-year-old girl named Margaret, daughter of German settlers, was gathering hickory nuts with her siblings. At some point she wandered away with her dog Penny and could not be found.

Her frantic parents and some neighbors searched through the night to no avail. The next day calls for volunteers went out to area towns and soon a force of 250 searchers were combing the woods day and night. The forest was lit by their torches and echoed with the ringing of bells and the calling of her name.

On the third day the tracks of the child and her dog were found and the searchers, energized by the discovery, intensified their efforts. However no further sign was found of her until the seventh day when her tracks were found again, this time minus those of her dog Penny. Several more days passed with no more tracks and by this time many of the discouraged searchers had gone home. Margaret's parents were in a state of grief. It seemed impossible that a child so young could survive in the Great Black Swamp wilderness fraught with wolves, bears, and wild hogs.

On the 11th day near the settlement of Portage, about 15 miles away, a couple of young men returned home after tracking down stray cattle in the woods. One of them asked his mother if Indian children had blue eyes. When she told him "no," he went on to explain that they had seen an Indian child in the woods with blue eyes speaking what they thought was an Indian tongue. They had given the child a biscuit which she had eaten quite rapidly. The group quickly realized this must be the lost girl Margaret and that the strange tongue she was speaking was probably her parents' native language of German.

A couple of members of the group hurried back into the woods and soon found her and brought her back to a cabin. That evening, news of the discovery reached her parents who spent the night with a mixture of joy and fear, fear that the report of Margaret being found would turn out to be untrue. Early the next morning Margaret's father arrived to an ecstatic reunion with her and took her home. The girl was hungry, dirty, and disoriented, but essentially all right.

The little girl could not tell much of her ordeal. But she did say that one night while sleeping a "big dog" took her dog Penny and killed him. The big dog was no doubt a wolf.

A TOWN CURSED?

In extreme southern Wood County near the Hancock County line lies the sleepy, railside hamlet of Bairdstown. Like thousands of small towns across America, Bairdstown never achieved the growth its founders dreamed of. However there were some who once believed a curse hung over Bairdstown's dreams.

Among the settlers living there prior to the official establishment of the town was an ornery man named Jim Slater. He was crude and mean and known to get into conflict with his neighbors. After one particularly sharp disagreement over payment for a wheat crop, Slater made threats that the owner of the wheat would never profit from it.

Weeks later an arsonist set fire to the wheat and stole some items from nearby barns. The unpopular Slater was the number one suspect and he was indicted and bound over to Wood County Common Pleas Court for trial. The only evidence against him was his threatening statements.

Slater protested his innocence and eventually was acquitted but ran up a considerable debt in attorney fees. With no money to pay, foreclosure proceedings on his land were initiated, which only added to his attorney debt. His property and possessions were sold at a sheriff's sale and Slater was left with nothing. His land was bought by a neighboring farmer named John Baird.

Just after the sale a broken Jim Slater shuffled into the Wood County Sheriff's office and sat slumped in a chair. Then, his anger rising, he raged against those involved in his prosecution and pronounced a curse on them. He also cursed John Baird, his former neighbor, who profited from his misfortune.

Baird laid out the town of Bairdstown on the land when the railroad came through and built a mill, hotel, and other buildings. For a while Baird and the town prospered, but then things began to go sour. The mill was torched by an arsonist and Baird ran into financial trouble and was subject to a number of lawsuits. Bankrupt, he eventually moved to Arkansas with his wife and daughter to run a hotel. There both his wife and daughter became ill and died.

The lawyer who represented Slater and later sued him for

payment also ran into his own financial troubles and lost his wife and only child to illness. The prosecuting attorney in the case went insane and died in an asylum.

Years after the incident a former neighbor of Slater's living in Kansas wrote a letter to the owner of the burned wheat explaining the incident that exonerated Slater completely. By then, of course, it was way too late. Jim Slater died broken and broke and was buried in the pauper's cemetery at the Wood County Infirmary.

THE MAIL MUST GO THROUGH

In the frontier days, government mail carriers had more to worry about than snow, rain, and the gloom of night to stay them from the swift completion of their appointed rounds. One of the earliest mail routes in northwest Ohio in the early 1830's was from Perrysburg to Lima and back. This route not only went through part of the Great Black Swamp, it also involved crossing the Blanchard River in Hancock County long before there were any bridges over it. It was a route with a high rate of carrier turnover.

One early carrier camping overnight somewhere in Wood County found himself being watched by a large number of wolves. To keep them at bay he built a roaring fire in front of a large hollow log while he took refuge inside. This worked for a while until the trunk caught fire, burning his face and hands and scorching the mail. That was his last run.

The next carrier made a couple of successful trips, then nearly drowned himself and his horse crossing the Blanchard River, losing the mail bag in the process. The waterlogged mailbag was found a few days later. However for the carrier it was his last trip.

Another carrier took the route in part because he wanted to see if the trip was as difficult as previous carriers had reported. While crossing the Blanchard his horse was crippled and he barely avoided being drowned. His curiosity satisfied, he resigned his post.

One of the more successful carriers on the Perrysburg to Lima route ran the route from February to November of 1832 with little incident. With the advent of winter, crossing the Blanchard

River became very hazardous and he frequently had to break through ice or slog through high water. On one occasion, he could not cross the swollen river despite numerous efforts and returned to Perrysburg. The government showed its gratitude for his efforts by withholding $50 from his pay.

TRAGEDY ON A WOOD COUNTY PRAIRIE

There was a pioneer named Valentine Sage in Wood County who, with his wife, was raising a family. Around the year 1852 his 13-year-old son became ill and died, which threw Sage into a state of depression.

His behavior became bizarre in the following months and he became obsessed with religious matters, frequently singing and praying in a loud voice. He began attending evening religious revivals in the old Plain Church a few miles west of Bowling Green, which served to stoke his religious fervor even more.

One snowy March morning after attending a revival, he arose early and went to his wife's bed and picked up their baby. She assumed he was taking the child to be warmed near the stove while she got dressed. Sage suddenly rushed outside and dashed the head of the child against the woodpile, killing it instantly. He then brought the dead child inside and presented it to his wife.

Afterward Sage seized an ax and forbade his wife and the remaining children from leaving the house while he sang and shouted religious songs and material. After a few hours his oldest daughter escaped and ran to a neighbor's home. The neighbor hurried to the home where Sage threatened to kill him if he so much as set foot on his property.

The neighbor left and returned with three other men and Sage stood in the doorway of his cabin with his ax threatening to kill anyone who tried to enter. Eventually one of the men climbed in through a window and sneaked up on Sage from behind while the others attacked from the front. Sage fought wildly and the men had to choke him into unconsciousness before they could finally subdue him.

Sage was tied up and locked in the county jail in Perrysburg where he died a time later, ranting and raving to the end. What became of his unfortunate wife and remaining children is not known.

Chapter XII:

FORT MEIGS, 1813

The role of Fort Meigs in the War of 1812 was a brief but intense one. When its builders began to chop away at the frozen ground of its site on a high bluff above the Maumee River in February, 1813, they probably never dreamed that its military importance would have already peaked by early August.

Of the several thousand soldiers who passed through Fort Meigs'gate, one was Captain Daniel Cushing who kept a diary. His writings give a glimpse of life in a frontier fort in harm's way. Many of Cushing's February and March entries while the fort was being built refer to the misery of living amidst mud or ice or both, depending on the temperature.

On March 9th several men were fired on outside the fort by Indians and one was struck, the bullet lodging in his Psalm book, thus saving him from injury. That same day a lieutenant from Pennsylvania who had gone duck hunting failed to return. The next day a search party found him, as Cushing wrote, "shot, tomahawked, and scalped. Also he was poked under the ice. He was brought into camp about 9 o'clock this morning and buried this afternoon."

As the month continued so did the mud and misery. "Our camp is overwhelmed with mud and water; my eyes never saw such a place for mankind to live," Cushing noted on the 18th. With all the nearby trees cut down to build the fort and no food to feed pack animals to haul wood from a distance, there were no fires to keep warm and illness was rampant. "Our men are very sickly; no wonder lying in mud or water and without fire; not less than two or three men die every day."

On March 20th Cushing, watching ice and water surging down the thawing Maumee River and floodplain, was amazed by the sight. "At this time this is the most romantic looking place that ever my eyes saw; to look from the battery on to the river and meadows is the greatest charm of any place that ever was in country that ever I traveled in; the water is gliding through the meadows swiftly and covered with all kinds of water fowl, and the ice which was left by the high water on the meadows is with out bounds three to fifteen feet deep..."

Near the end of the month a private, probably frustrated by the conditions he was living in, threatened to blow up the fort's ammunition and defect to the British, much to his later regret. He was court-martialed and sentenced "to be confined, tied to a post or log in a tent by himself one month, to have a handcuff on his right hand, to ride a wooden horse 30 minutes once a week for one month with a six pound ball fastened to each foot, to wear a ball and chain the whole time, to have one eye brow and one side of his head shaved and to be fed bread and water only." After this the private was kicked out of the army.

March flowed into April and the building of Fort Meigs was nearly completed. With the improving weather came increasing fear of attack. On April 14th Cushing noted "We are expecting the British and Indians to attack us every night." That same night a nervous sentry shot a horse, thinking it was an Indian. General William Henry Harrison was now in command of Fort Meigs and reinforcements and supplies were pouring into the fort as a major confrontation with the British was expected. By the end of the month, the British and Tecumseh-led Indians were massing on the opposite side of the river.

On May 1st British bombardment of the fort began in earnest while the cannons in Fort Meigs thundered in reply. On May 2nd Cushing wrote, "This morning they commenced a heavy fire from all their batteries both with cannonade and bombs and our camp is completely surrounded with Indians and British keeping up a heavy fire of musketry and rifles. They threw at us this day about 350 shot, a large portion of them red hot." The British heated the cannonballs hoping to ignite the fort's powder magazines. The burning, hissing shells that literally boiled in the ground when they landed only added to the fear of the soldiers in the fort

The next day the bombardment continued and over 500 shells came screaming into the fort. Traverses, protective mounds of earth, ran the length of the fort and along its wings keeping the loss of life minimal, considering the volume of fire. One soldier became adept at identifying by a shell's sound where it would land and shouting out a warning to that part of the fort. Then came a shell whose sound left him standing frozen, a quizzical look on his face. An instant later that missile landed on him, sending him to his eternal reward.

The British continued pouring shells into the fort for several days while the Americans, with less ammunition to spare, fired back more deliberately. While the sound of cannons thundered up and down the Maumee Valley, Indians crept close enough to send in volleys of musket fire both from the ground and from high in nearby trees. The fort too well-fortified to charge, the Indians had tried a number of ruses to get the Americans to leave the safety of its walls and fight, something they had no intention of doing.

On May 5th a reinforcing army of 1,200 Kentucky soldiers coming downriver neared the fort. A detachment of 800 under a Colonel Dudley was to first attack and disable the British cannons across the river and beat a hasty retreat to the safety of Fort Meigs. Their mission completed, the excited soldiers instead fell for an Indian ruse and chased them into the woods. There they were surrounded and in what became known as Dudley's Defeat, 650 were killed or captured. Captain Cushing and the other soldiers could only watch helplessly from the fort. Afterward, a massacre of the captives ensued at old Fort Miamis, a slaughter stopped by Tecumseh.

On May 6th Cushing noted. "This day no fighting. A complete cessation of arms on both sides." Indeed the discouraged British and Indians were giving up as General Harrison's "hunker down" strategy had worked, although the Americans had paid a price. In addition to the Dudley debacle there were nearly 80 dead to bury and 200 wounded to treat inside the fort. On the 9th, a battle-numbed Cushing walked about the grounds outside Fort Meigs where more dead from both sides lay. "The sight of dead men has become no more terrifying than the sight of dead flies on a summer day," he wrote.

The next couple of weeks were spent recovering British cannon and shot left behind by the British and burying 45 of Colonel Dudley's men found at Fort Miamis. On May 17th Cushing observed, "Fine weather this morning, my men in high spirits, fish plenty, no want of provisions, all that is wanting to have things complete is a little whiskey. I took sail in a small canoe this morning and caught 62 white bass that would weigh one pound each...caught them with a hook and a line baited with a red rag."

The next six weeks or so were generally uneventful, although death continued to be a regular visitor. There were victims of lingering battle wounds and a measles and mumps outbreak to bury, and the soldiers continued to strengthen the fort in the event of another attack.

Late in June Captain Cushing discovered that the high bluff where Fort Meigs stood had known human bloodshed before. "I have spent several hours in walking myself around the garrison both outside of the pickets and inside of the batteries. I find by examination that this place must have been a seat of war for ages past.

"In almost every place where we have thrown up the earth we find human bones aplenty. Yesterday the fatigue party that were digging a trench in front of blockhouse No. 3 and 4 came upon a pile of bones where they took out 25 skulls in one pit...In walking around this garrison on the earth that has been thrown up it was like walking on the sea shore upon mussel shells, only in this case human bones."

As June melted into July the soldiers in the fort began to tense again in light of reports that the Indians and British were preparing for another siege. In recent weeks there had been a number of skirmishes with Indians resulting in casualties on both sides. Meanwhile Cushing had taken ill, fighting fever and nausea.

On July 20th this was confirmed. "At 9 o'clock this evening it is reported that two sails were seen on the river about sundown. It is expected the British and Indians are coming to pay us another visit."

The next day the second siege of Fort Meigs began, but it was a half-hearted effort compared to the first. On July 26th Cushing wrote, "this is the sixth day of the siege and not a man killed except what were killed at the picket guard the first day." On that same day the sound of heavy gunfire was heard about a mile away and there was serious concern among the American command that a relief expedition on its way to the fort was in deep trouble. Just about then "there came up the heaviest thunder shower that ever I experienced. I am positive I never in all my life saw it rain harder than it did for nearly one hour; our camp was completely inundated."

Guns on both sides fell silent as the second siege of Fort Meigs had, in effect, been rained out. The sounds of gunfire, it turned out, had been yet another Indian ruse designed to lure the Americans out and, once again, they hadn't taken the bait. By July 31st the Indian warriors and British soldiers were long gone, never to return to the Maumee Valley.

July 31st is also when Cushing's diary comes to an abrupt end. His last lines were "I am very unwell this evening with fevers and chills. The watchword this night is Tennessee." Perhaps the pages from that point on were lost or perhaps, with the fort no longer being a military target, he felt no need to continue his chronicle. Captain Daniel Cushing survived the bombs and bullets at Fort Meigs in the War of 1812. However it is believed that on his journey back to his native Massachusetts, he was involved in an accident in which he drowned.

Exterior view of the reconstructed Fort Meigs in Perrysburg.

Interior view of Fort Meigs. The mound of earth, or traverse, visible on the left helped protect the soldiers in the fort from heavy British bombardment.

Chapter XIII:

A FROG TOWN WITH A HOGBACK

In the beginning there was Port Lawrence and Vistula, two riverside towns on the Maumee River about a mile apart. Port Lawrence was centered about where the intersection of Monroe and Summit streets is today while Vistula was similarly situated at what is now the intersection of Summit and Lagrange streets.

Dividing the villages was a sort of no man's land, a 15 to 20-foot high, forested ridge called a hogback that ran along the Maumee River and today's Summit Street and scene of Saturday night fist fights between boys from the rival villages. The east side of the hogback sloped to a marshy area and the river, while the west side descended to Mud Creek, a generous name for what was actually a stagnant body of swampy water blessed with a current only after a heavy rain. From Mud Creek more marsh extended north and west to as far as where 10th Street is today.

In 1833 Port Lawrence and Vistula put their differences aside and agreed to work together as one and in 1836 they petitioned the state government in Columbus for city status. On January 7, 1837 Toledo was officially born, just in time for the financial panic of 1837 and resulting Depression. This was followed by the Drought of 1838, which killed crops, withered trees, and even dried up parts of the Great Black Swamp.

Toledo almost immediately earned the nickname Frog Town,

a moniker spurred in part by the legions of frogs leaping through the city during the 1838 drought from dried up marshlands seeking the moisture of the Maumee River. Frog legs were a regular "special of the day" at the local hotel dining rooms and Toledo was treated nightly to concerts in frog flat from the croaking of tens of thousands of the green-skinned amphibians. In addition, the city's swampy conditions led to the multiple marsh maladies of mosquitoes, malaria, mud, and miasma.

Summers brought clouds of mosquitoes bearing a variety of malarial, swamp fevers that branded Toledo a sickly place to live, "Death Valley" in the eyes of some. Under certain atmospheric conditions decaying swamp vegetation led to malodorous clouds or "miasma" that settled over the town and led locals to shut their windows tight at night. And the mud could be profuse after a heavy rain. Regional newspapers liked to tease the city by printing tales of horses and buggies and even whole trains sinking into the mud and out of sight.

If by 1846 Toledo was making progress as a vital new community and a desirable place to live, it certainly was lost on a Methodist minister visiting that year. Writing in the *Nashville Christian Advocate*, he minced no words : "Toledo is a new town at the mouth of the Maumee River. Of all the new towns I ever saw, I think it is the most miserable. The unfinished houses without windows, chimneys, or cellars, and many of them deserted of tenantry, are falling to decay."

The good reverend continued. "The place is so sickly that few will consent to stay here except blacklegs (swindlers) and desperadoes...A few human shadows, yellow as the autumn forests around them, creep shivering through the muddy streets, or lurk about the steamboat landing, and live by borrowing and chewing tobacco. Our hotel seemed to be the general rendezvous of bedbugs for all the western country and for breakfast they gave us hash of which I should not dare guess the ingredients. Here the philosopher might well light his lamp at noon to find an honest man."

Obviously the local chamber of commerce, if any such group existed at the time, had its work cut out.

Meanwhile, the hogback that divided the former villages of

Port Lawrence and Vistula remained a challenge. Summit Street apparently was channeled into this ridge as one historian said the street, "at this point resembled a canal with the water drained out." A plank walkway laid on the north side of Summit Street could be precarious, according to the same observer; "In rainy weather that sidewalk was subject to landslides and became a very uncertain means of communication."

The challenges of navigating early Summit Street moved one local resident to poetry, as recorded in the *Toledo Daily Blade* in December, 1852, that went in part:

> *O'er Summit Street, whee'er I cast my eyes,*
> *What curious thought along my senses creep.*
> *Napoleon crossed the Alps; his high emprise,*
> *Won him a deathless name, but not a step.*
> *Of all the peaks he crossed, so hard to rise,*
> *As Summit street, beneath whose lowest deep.*
> *There is a depth no mortal ever scanned*
> *A gloomy deep of mud devoid of sand."*

It was clear that Toledo's physical oddities, swampy lowland interrupted by a sharp ridge dividing the city's waterfront, would have to be addressed. After a series of cholera epidemics that began in 1849, aggravated in part by the city's marshy real estate, the *Toledo Daily Blade* editorialized in 1854, "We must bid adieu to the frogs and the tadpoles and eat no more of the delicious mud-turtle soup manufactured out of the denizens of that unsightly swamp-hole...The time will come when Mud Creek will be forgotten in our history." It was around this time that plans for sewers and drainage began in earnest and Toledo slowly emerged from the swamp.

It was also around this time that excavation and grading began on the hogback. The earth from this was used to fill the marshes on the Maumee River side of the ridge which led to the construction of Water Street and its docks and warehouses. The once separate waterfronts of Port Lawrence and Vistula were finally joined by a mile-long harbor and the existence of the hogback was soon forgotten. Only Summit Street's name reminds that it was not always the level thoroughfare it is today.

However when the Lucas County Courthouse was designed in the 1890's its planners felt that Toledo's amphibious heritage should, in some small way, be preserved. Thus Toledo may be home to the only courthouse in the country with a floor tile mosaic of a frog staring up at visitors.

This tile mosaic of a frog in the Adams Street entrance of the Lucas County Courthouse reminds visitors of Toledo's swampy heritage.

Chapter XIV:

SUMMERS OF DREAD

Of all the heartbreaks endured by early northwest Ohio residents perhaps the cruelest one was cholera epidemics. It was also the one that left them gripped in fear, not knowing the cause of the disease or how it spread. For the highly contagious cholera struck quickly and mercilessly, at times taking the life a healthy person in a matter of hours.

The disease's symptoms were gruesome; almost uncontrollable vomiting and diarrhea and dramatic changes in skin color. So great was the fear of cholera that incidents of family members fleeing, leaving ill loved ones to die, were not uncommon. Even the slightest hint of symptoms was enough to send a person into full-blown panic and fright certainly contributed to some deaths.

A very aggressive bacterial infection, cholera thrives amidst poor sanitary conditions and hot weather and spreads through personal contact and contaminated water. Its roots reach to ancient India and for centuries it was a plague known in that part of the world. In 1832, it crossed the Atlantic on an immigrant ship heading for Quebec. From there it traveled down the St. Lawrence River valley to New York and brushed northwest Ohio before it ran its course.

The first major northwest Ohio cholera epidemic literally floated ashore in 1834 when dead victims were tossed off a cholera-wracked troop transport sailing for Detroit, their bodies washing up along the Marblehead peninsula. Local residents, believing them to be victims of a shipwreck, dragged them ashore to give them a proper burial. This act of charity proved to be deadly as cholera cut through the Marblehead village and peninsula, taking the lives of half its residents. From there it spread to Sandusky, Fremont, and Tiffin.

The next widespread outbreak occurred in 1849, the beginning of a five-year period of episodic cholera outbreaks, and spread across the country. Northwest Ohio was not spared. Sandusky had it the worst that year and as July drew to a close, daily death tolls of 30 or more were common and the city was having trouble finding enough men to dig the graves. In addition, panic set in and thousands of residents fled the city, some never to return. At one point only 2,000 persons remained out of a population of over 5,000.

By the time the epidemic waned in September, over 400 Sandusky residents had lost their lives in just over two months including government officials, members of the clergy, and physicians. Local physician Dr. Charles Cochrane was the only doctor on duty at one point in the epidemic until additional doctors arrived from out of town. After the plague subsided he wrote that he became so numbed by all the death at the height of the scourge that he experienced less emotion seeing people die than he had previously felt seeing animals die in a slaughterhouse.

Many victims of the Sandusky epidemic were buried in a cemetery near downtown, including an unknown number in a common trench, the multitude of dead and the urgency to bury them being so great. Now known as The Cholera Cemetery, a 15-foot tall memorial shaft rises over unmarked graves, ground where grief hung like a veil in the summer of 1849. A marker at the cemetery notes "dismay stalked abroad in the daytime and the drowsy night was hideous with the wailings of the disconsolate."

The 1849 cholera epidemic also spread to Toledo, showing up initially in an Irish boarding house in mid-July. Its voracious nature was amply demonstrated in the death of the Toledo postmaster who became ill at 10 a.m. on July 30 and was dead by 7 p.m. that evening. The epidemic lasted about a month until mid-August, during which the city pretty much shut down. About eighty people died, substantially less than Sandusky's and a mere trifle compared to the nearly 6,000 who died in Cincinnati that year.

Toledo and northwest Ohio were hit again by lesser cholera outbreaks in 1850 and 1852 with the year 1854 capping off a deadly five-year span. June melted uneventfully into early July that year until a steamer from Buffalo docked, discharging passengers and the dreaded disease. The epidemic took root in East Toledo, then called Utah, and at one point 34 died there in a three-day period. People fled, only to return after being refused shelter in nearby towns by residents fearful of the disease.

One story that circulated concerned an unscrupulous undertaker who had contracted with the city to bury victims who had no family or friends to do so. To increase his profits he dumped the bodies in an open grave in the country in order to reuse the same coffin. Going about his duties he happened across a the body of a man lying in the street, gathered him up, and so disposed of him. When he returned later that day he found the man sitting on a fence, utterly confused as to how he had gotten there. For he merely had been sleeping off a drunk and was anxious to get back to town to pick up where he had left off.

The plague swept up the Maumee Valley and Perrysburg was particularly hard hit. At the height of the scourge less than half the village's population of 1,800 remained in the town and the only activities going on were caring for the sick and burying the dead. The fear of outsiders bringing in the disease was so great that the bridge between Perrysburg and Maumee was guarded at night.

The 1854 epidemic ran its course by the end of August and in Toledo alone there were an estimated 400 dead, a significant toll in a city with a population of about 8,000. Perrysburg buried around 120 of its own. And all through northwest Ohio gravestones bearing dates from the summer of 1854 can be found.

One beneficial development to come out of the summer of 1854 was the discovery by a British physician that demonstrated a positive link between contaminated public water supplies and the spread of cholera. Toledo and cities everywhere began to rethink their water delivery systems and upgrade their rudimentary sewers. Never again would the dark cloud of cholera sweep across the land.

The Cholera Cemetery in Sandusky, Ohio. Over 400 Sandusky residents died from the disease in the summer of 1849.

Chapter XV:

THE CANAL DAYS

I've got a mule and her name is Sal;
Fifteen miles on the Erie Canal.
She's a good old worker and a good old pal;
Fifteen miles on the Erie Canal."

So went one of the more popular songs of the canal days sung by boatmen as they guided their long flat crafts down narrow channels of lazy, muddy waters. While the canal of the song was the Albany to Buffalo waterway in New York, it no doubt echoed along the towpaths of the Miami and Erie Canal where it slanted through northwest Ohio.

When the Erie Canal in New York opened in 1825 to tremendous fanfare—it was a feat of unparalleled engineering at the time and called the eighth wonder of the world—canal fever swept the country and Ohio was no exception.

The Miami Canal linking Cincinnati and Dayton opened in 1829 and enjoyed considerable financial success, spurring plans for a link to Toledo and Lake Erie. However the link to Toledo took much longer than expected. There was the usual political bickering that goes with any major project. A ridge in west central Ohio 400 feet above the level of Lake Erie had to be conquered with a series of locks and reservoirs. The removal of the earth along the canal route, done primarily by spade, shovel, and sweat, was painfully slow. And the canal workers, mostly Irish immigrants who lived in filthy conditions in canal-side shanties, were subject to disease and death so much that construction was suspended in the summer months.

In 1843 the Wabash and Erie Canal opened and in May a canal boat from Lafayette, Indiana became the first to glide through northwest Ohio. Escorting the mule-drawn barge along its way were the shouts of children, the barking of dogs, and looks of amazement from farmers and townsfolk alike. On May 8th it arrived in Toledo near the junction of Swan Creek and Summit Street and virtually the whole town was there. Bells rang, guns were fired, a band played, and thousands cheered. The boat's crew was taken to a local hotel and royally wined and dined. For sure to follow that boat down those muddy canal waters was great economic growth and prosperity, or so everyone believed.

In 1845 the Miami Extension Canal was completed linking the northern and southern tiers of the state and the waterway was named the Miami and Erie Canal. The first boat from Cincinnati arrived in Toledo in June and northwest Ohio's canal era was in full swing. Between 1845 and 1849 the number of bushels of corn shipped through Toledo rose from 30,000 to over two million.

As many as fifty of the long, narrow canal boats, both freighters and passenger boats, or "packets," might be docked in Toledo at any one time. Passengers, both local and from as far away as New York City, embarked and disembarked at the Swan Creek docks.

A journey down the canal on a packet could be a mixed bag. Daytime travel in nice weather was pretty good as passengers could lounge on deck and watch the passing countryside unfold, get a drink in the bar, or stretch their legs by walking along the towpath.

On the other hand nights could be a little tough as the boats were often overcrowded, especially during periods of heavy immigrant movement west. Passengers slept below decks with little or no privacy in tiers of canvas bunks hung from the walls, the bunk above often sagging inches above the person sleeping below. There was little ventilation and upon waking in the morning travelers would scurry above deck, at times gasping for fresh air.

In the early days some of the canal boat crews could be a rough bunch as boats approaching a lock from opposite directions followed a very basic method of deciding which boat received priority. The crews would shout "whose lock is this," and leap off their boats and beat the heck out of each other. The crew still standing at the end got to "lock through" first. Hard drinking and even harder swearing only added to the "color" of the crews.

Over time conditions on packets improved as operators realized that attending to the comfort and enjoyment of their passengers was good for business. And the placid waters of the canal provided a smoother, more relaxing means of travel than could any horse.

By around 1850 just as canals were hitting their stride as a major economic and social force, a different kind of horse, the iron horse, came into play. Railroads, which were easier to build, could go almost anywhere, could operate the year around, and whose trains went faster, became the new transportation darling of the country.

In the 1850's Ohio laid more miles of track than any other state, sending the Miami and Erie Canal on a slow float into transportation history. By 1858 the canal extension into Indiana was in disuse and totally abandoned by 1888, while use of the rest of the canal varied by region.

Ohio's canals, including the Miami and Erie, enjoyed a brief resurgence after they underwent considerable reconstruction and improvement by the state during the period of 1906 to 1909. However the tremendous spring floods of 1913 did substantial damage and proved to be the final blow to the Miami and Erie Canal.

On July 6, 1929 government dignitaries and a crowd gathered at the Providence Mill lock at Grand Rapids to mark the official closing of the Miami and Erie, and to herald the highways that would be built in its place. Speeches were given, aerial bombs were rocketed into the air, and a fleet of aircraft dipped its wings as the great lock gates were closed for the final time. However some unknown person had blown open a hole in the side of the canal several days earlier near Waterville, sending its waters gushing to the Maumee River. So on its final official day only a trickle of water flowed along the bed of the Miami and Erie Canal, a fitting end.

The canal boat Turtle glides down the Miami and Erie Canal in Maumee in this 1904 photo. (Photo courtesy of the History and Genealogy Department, Toledo-Lucas County Public Library).

Chapter XVI:

EARLY JOURNEY THROUGH NORTHWEST OHIO

It was a sleepy mid-July day in the summer of 1812 in the then Ohio capital of Chillicothe when an urgent message arrived for Governor Meigs. It was from General William Hull, an aging Revolutionary War general, who had recently marched his army to Detroit to defend it from the British in the early days of the War of 1812. It seemed that upon reaching Maumee Bay he had foolishly loaded the majority of his army's provisions onto a schooner to be transported the rest of the way only to have that ship promptly seized by the British.

Now, very short of supplies, General Hull was asking Governor Meigs to send a relief expedition with more provisions. The next morning Governor Meigs called a town meeting asking for volunteers, hoping to avoid the time-consuming and tedious process of raising a company via the draft. Ninety-five Chillicothe citizens responded, from mechanics to merchants to lawyers, and within 48 hours were ready to march. Their mission was not only to take supplies to Detroit but to then join Hull's army and fight.

They left Chillicothe on July 21st for Urbana, Ohio where they would pick up the supplies. Among the volunteer soldiers was a private by the name of C. Williams who wrote letters to his wife and kept a journal. The three-day march to Urbana in hot weather carrying thirty-pound packs left the green citizen-soldiers whipped. Sleeping on bare ground at night with no tent instead of in their accustomed Chillicothe beds, and rotating nightly guard duty only added to their fatigue. Williams wrote his wife from Urbana "My limbs were so stiff and sore at the end of each day's march I could hardly walk."

They rested a couple of days at Urbana then left with their supplies; 70 pack horses each loaded with 200 pounds of flour and 300 head of beef cattle. A couple of days later they arrived at Fort McArthur, near the present town of Kenton. Williams again wrote his wife from there, obviously feeling stronger. "I am very well, in good spirits and much improved in strength and general health. The fatigues and hardships of a soldier's life are just what I needed. You would not believe it possible for me to endure what I daily undergo in common with fellow soldiers."

Williams went on to describe their trail cuisine, which consisted of flour, bacon, and salt. "You would smile at our mode of cooking, could you see us thus employed," he penned. "Our food is coarse and cooked in the roughest manner." The flour was kneaded into long rolls of dough which were coiled around six-foot poles and baked over an open fire while the bacon, stuck to the ends of twigs, was cooked in a similar manner.

"Each man then takes a piece of the pole-bread and lays thereon a piece of bacon and with his knife cuts there from and eats his meal with a good appetite," Williams wrote. "Enough is thus cooked each night to serve for the next day." And the water they drank was a bit less than fresh. "For whole days together we have had to use water from stagnant ponds and wagon ruts and horse tracks in the road."

From Fort McArthur the expedition continued north, following the wagon tracks left by Hull's army that came to be known as Hull's Trace, a forerunner to many modern roads. The expedition reached Fort Findlay on the Blanchard River, traveling on what would later become Main Street in Findlay.

From Fort Findlay it was north to the Great Black Swamp. Traveling the Swamp in mid-summer was to see it at its best, for it was at its driest and its foliage at its fullest. And Private Williams, who obviously had a keen eye for nature's beauty, thoroughly enjoyed what he saw. After passing through the Swamp and reaching the east bank of the Maumee River on

August 3rd Williams wrote, "the country we passed through yesterday is the most delightful I have ever seen." He went on to describe groves of hickory and oak trees rising out of "natural plains of many miles in extent, apparently as level as the ocean."

An exuberant Williams reported "these plains are covered with a most luxuriant growth of grass and herbs and an endless variety of beautiful native flowers—Cardinal Flower, Lady of the Lake, Blue Flag, Honeysuckles, Red Lobelia, Wild Fox-Glove, Wild Iris, and Wild Columbine, representing all the colors of the rainbow and loading the atmosphere with their perfume...What a rich field this is for the botanist!"

Indeed," Williams continued, "I had almost imagined that (18th century English poet Thomas) Gray must have seen this plain before he penned his inimitable 'Elegy' and that it was in reference to it he wrote these beautiful lines:

> For many a flower is born to blush unseen
> And waste its sweetness on the desert air."
> From *Elegy Written in A Country Churchyard*

The expedition remained on the Maumee River several days, awaiting reinforcements from Cleveland and Sandusky, and camping on the site of the Battle of Fallen Timbers before moving down river below the old British Fort Miamis. During the layover Williams wrote of the beauty of the Maumee River: "the descent of the current over successive ledges of rock form beautiful little cascades at distances of a few yards in between...Near our encampment, in the bank of the river, is a large spring of pure, cold water which is very refreshing after drinking, as we very often did, from puddles in the road."

While in Maumee the expedition received orders from General Hull to proceed to the Raisin River near present-day Monroe, Mich., and await a detachment from Detroit to escort them the rest of the way. The band headed north, continuing on Hull's Trace, traveling over what is Detroit Avenue in Toledo today, and Private William's writings from that point are concerned not with nature and beauty but with mankind and war.

By the time the expedition reached the Raisin River, things

were going very badly for the American forces in Detroit, as the Chillicothe group would soon learn. After some forays into Canada, General Hull and his army had retreated to Fort Detroit and were faced by a larger British army combined with an Indian force led by the legendary Shawnee Chief Tecumseh. British troops also occupied the land between Detroit and the Raisin River, cutting off the supply route. Hull sent several sorties from Detroit to reach the supply expedition but all were turned back.

On August 11th Williams wrote to Governor Meigs, "It is certain that our affairs on the frontier wear a very serious and gloomy prospect. All communication between us and Detroit has been several days wholly cut off by the enemy." Three days later he wrote, "All thought of being able to proceed to Detroit is now abandoned and our attention is turned exclusively to fortifying our position and putting it in the best state of defense that we can."

Indeed the small supply expedition was in a perilous position as an enemy army many times its size was only a few hours march away. An increasingly fearful Williams noted that if the British attacked them with artillery, "our rotten stockade will be battered to the ground in ten minutes. What our fate will be I cannot tell...We have lost all confidence in General Hull."

On August 16th, in what remains a low point in American military history and one described as "so extraordinary, so astonishing" by Williams, General Hull surrendered Detroit and all the forces under his command to the British without a fight. He feared that a battle would result in massive American casualties and possible atrocities by the Indians. A British captain arrived at the Raisin River and presented papers to the Chillicothe party informing them of the above and, that under the terms of the surrender, they were prisoners of war.

They refused to believe it. The only logical explanation it seemed was that the papers were forged and that the captain was a spy. The British officer was seized and placed under guard. However some American soldiers who had escaped from Detroit arrived and confirmed the ignominious end of the American forces there.

Now the expedition had a decision to make; surrender as per General Hull's orders or flee back to Ohio. A council was held and it was unanimously decided to go back. They released the British captain and the expedition left at 10 P.M. that night under a dark and moonless sky, the muddy ruts of the road serving as their only guide. They soon were pursued by Tecumseh leading a force of several hundred Indians along with some British regulars.

By the next morning they had reached the Maumee River where the exhausted group was fed a little food by local residents and continued on. What had been an orderly and, for Williams, enjoyable, trek through the Great Black Swamp a few weeks before had become a desperate flight for life. They marched that day until midnight and slept leaning against a tree or any other dry place they could find. About noon the next day they made it to Fort Findlay and probable safety for it was unlikely Tecumseh would carry his pursuit that far. In fact, it is believed the Shawnee chief and his army marched only as far as the Maumee River before returning to Detroit.

Not taking any chances, the expedition paused at Fort Findlay just long enough to eat and hurried on for two more days until completely out of Indian country, where they proceeded at a more leisurely pace back to Chillicothe. They arrived home on August 23, 1812 after an absence of nearly five weeks without the loss of a man. And even though they were never held, they were recognized as having been prisoners of war and credited by Governor Meigs for having served a full tour of duty.

·What became of Private Williams is not known, only that his remarkable writings survive. General Hull was court martialed and sentenced to death, but later, in light of his years of service during the Revolution, was pardoned by President James Madison . The following spring William Henry Harrison built Fort Meigs in Perrysburg from which he and his army swept the British and Indians out of the western Lake Erie theater, culminating at the Battle of Thames in Ontario in October. It was there that Tecumseh breathed his last. Never again would northwest Ohio or southeast Michigan be visited by war.

Chapter XVII:

THE FEARLESS TRAVELER

Another early traveler through the Black Swamp was an adventurer named Estwick Evans, a New Englander who set off to see the country in 1818. He left his small New Hampshire town in February on the first leg of his journey which would take him to Detroit. Lying in his path was the Great Black Swamp.

He arrived at the eastern edge of the Swamp around the first of March, wearing heavy clothes made from skins of buffalo, bear, and deer, and carrying baggage. His destination, some 40 miles away, was the west edge of the Swamp and Fort Meigs. While mosquitoes and fever were not a problem that time of year, icy waist-to-chest deep water was.

Surveying the Swamp as he embarked on his journey he described it as being "in its very worst state. There was a unusual quantity of snow and ice on the ground and the weather being moderate, the water rapidly increased."

On the first day he ran into an Indian near the Sandusky River and asked for "some information as to the best way through this trackless wild, but he either could not speak English, or pretended this was the case. It is said they frequently do so."

Evan's continued on and his next human encounter was, to say the least, on the bizarre side. He soon came across three Indians in the company of a drunken white man. The white man had agreed to do some work for the Indians but had instead had run away and the Indians were returning with him.

While Evans was obtaining directions from the Indians, the white man, who had slipped away from the group a bit, took off running. "My rifle was immediately seized by the Indians for the purpose of shooting him but by great exertions I held it until the man was out of sight, and then they desisted and pursued him."

Evans marched on, leaving the Indians to chase their recalcitrant employee, and found a high spot and stopped for the night. Did sleeping on the ground, alone and deep in a vast, semi-frozen swamp induce feelings of fear or want? Hardly.

"My little fire appeared like a star of the bosom of heaven," Evans wrote. "Earth was my couch and my covering the brilliant canopy of heaven...How great are the advantages of solitude! How sublime is the silence of nature's ever active energies! There is something in the very name of wilderness which charms the ear and soothes the spirit of man. There is religion in it."

Evans slept soundly that starry night, waking to a lowering sky and continuing on, rain now his traveling companion. Around mid-day he came to the swollen Portage River, its banks overflowing on both sides for a quarter mile. With some difficulty he managed to locate the channel of the river and floated across on a large log, navigating a rapid current and icy waters.

When he got to the other side the water was up to his shoulders. "Here I stopped to survey my situation. Although the trees were large and scattering, I could not perceive the land." He decided to recross the river and try another location but could not find his log. "I was here completely bewildered. Alone, nearly up to my neck in water, apparently in the midst of a shoreless ocean..."

Fear if not abject despair might seem to be the logical response in such a situation, but not for this intrepid Black Swamp traveler. "My situation was rather unpleasant," wrote Evans in a bit of an understatement, but "the novelty of it, however, together with my apparent inability to extricate myself produced a resourceless smile." Evans, along with his resourceless smile, finally did manage "by much labour and with great hazard" to safely reach the western shore of the river where he spent the night.

The next day the temperature dropped and icicles formed on Evans clothes as he journeyed on. Ice formed upon the water but not of sufficient strength to support his weight. It was an arduous day of travel, the water being three to four feet deep most of the way, "but my Buffalo pantaloons were a defence against the thick yet brittle ice through which I was continually breaking."

At night he camped on a rise with a group of 20 Wyandot Indians. "Their condition was deplorable," Evans wrote. "They had, the day before, buried one of their company, another of them was very sick and they had no provisions. I had but a trifle myself and the wants of the sick Indian rendered me supperless."

The night was very cold and Evans, being quite wet, was unable to sleep, a layer of bark the only thing keeping him off the ground. One of the Indians spoke English and he and Evans spoke at length about the Great Spirit. Most of the Indians were also unable to sleep and they sang tribal songs, Evans listening by the light of a smoky fire.

At dawn of the next day Evans arose and traveled the rest of the way to Fort Meigs. There he rested only an hour before continuing on to Detroit.

Chapter XVIII:

BLACK SWAMP GAS AND BLACK GOLD

Like a shooting star, a natural gas industry blazed over the placid plains of the former Great Black Swamp in the mid-1880's and early 1890's And much like a shooting star, it came suddenly, burned brilliantly, and was gone quickly.

For decades, early settlers knew about the presence of a mysterious and flammable gas. There were stories of Indian ceremonies being conducted around flaming ground, seeping gas that had been ignited with a torch. Farmers digging wells for water at times encountered sulfurous natural gas which led them to turn up their noses and dig elsewhere. Even those who realized that gas could be burned might run some through a pipe or tube and ignite it, merely to amuse their friends. Gas was looked at both as an annoyance and a curiosity.

Then came the drilling of the first oil well in the summer of 1859 in Western Pennsylvania, an event that would change the world. Soon it was realized that the natural gas that was found in oil wells was itself a viable fuel and by the 1870's many of Pittsburgh's great factories had converted to natural gas.

The developing technology, along with dwindling stocks of gas in the Pennsylvania fields, brought the quest for fuel to northwestern Ohio and in the early 1880's exploration began in earnest. In December, 1884 on a quiet farm south of Findlay a handful of people watched as the newly-formed Findlay Natural Gas Company struck a large field of natural gas 1,000 feet below the surface. From that point the fever was on.

As the word spread, test wells were drilled all over northwest Ohio. Spurring the activity was the belief that an enormous pool of gas lay under the area, a pool that could be tapped if only one drilled deep enough. Even more erroneous was the belief that natural gas was a renewable resource, that deep in the bowels of the earth the interaction of carbon, salt water, and intense heat created gas. And in a classic case of believing what you want to believe, many thought that the more gas that was used the more that would be generated, that the supply was, in effect, infinite.

In addition to the above myths, there were real advantages of natural gas over wood and coal, the predominant fuels of the day, that made it so alluring. Gas burned cleanly, wood and coal did not; gas flowed freely from the ground, wood and coal did not; and gas, it was believed, would cost next to nothing, wood and coal did not. Gas was, said its promoters, the "perfect fuel."

Early test wells in Toledo and other locations produced little. However on January 20, 1886 the village of Findlay literally shook as an enormous deposit of gas was struck almost in the middle of town, shooting flames over 100 feet in the air. Known as the Karg well, it burned wildly for four months before it could be brought under control, a raging, thundering inferno that could be heard five miles away and seen as far away as Toledo at night under the right atmospheric conditions.

A reporter for the now-defunct *Toledo News Bee* wrote: "Five or six miles before reaching Findlay a brilliant light is seen in the heavens and a mile or two further discloses to the vision a great cloud of fire. This was the great Karg well. Its proportion, intensity, and grandeur increase as the town is neared when church steeples and housetops are brought out with the distinctiveness of day."

The discovery of a second large Hancock County well led Toledo to think less about drilling and more about constructing pipelines to transport the gaseous gold north. Plans were made in Toledo for two competing pipelines in order to keep rates down while Hancock County had more gas than it knew what to do with and wells burned night and day. Uniting all northwest Ohio communities was an underlying conviction that an infinite supply of free-flowing natural gas was going to bring about unparalleled economic prosperity.

In June, 1887 gas was discovered in Waterville and piped to Toledo. The following month crowds cheered when a six-inch gas standpipe was ignited near the Cherry Street Bridge in East Toledo. In September, a "Grand Gas Celebration" was held and flames reflected in 25,000 pairs of eyes as the roaring blaze of a dozen standpipes towering 100 feet in the air turned night into day.

Civic confidence ran wild as evidenced in a *Toledo Daily Blade* editorial the following day: "Toledo, the queen city of the lakes, goes forth conquering, one hand bearing a torch with light for the world, with fire for a nation's forges, with heat for a million homes, with fuel for thousands of factories; the other holding cheap iron, lumber, copper, oil, wheat and wool."

Indeed the optimism was not confined to the local media as newspapers in both Columbus and Cleveland referred to Toledo as "the Future Great" in headlines reporting the gas celebration.

That same summer Findlay held a three-day celebration of its own, the city by then bulging with speculators, investors, and industrialists. Fifty-eight decorative arches soared over city streets with flames streaming from burning natural gas jets and bearing banners telling of the town's new-found fortune. "Thirty-One Factories Located Within One Year" and "Findlay, the Center of the World," boasted a couple. But the one that might have had the most appeal was "Women Split No Wood in Findlay."

It was a heady time in northwest Ohio and perhaps the industry most drawn by the promise of cheap or free gas was the glass industry and its furnaces needing large amounts of fuel. Fostoria saw the beginning of a glass industry there that over time counted 13 factories before it ran its course. A number of glass factories relocated to Bowling Green leading that town to be dubbed "The Crystal City." The Libbey Glass Company relocated from New England to Toledo in 1888 and remains a major employer today. And real estate values in Toledo and other northwest Ohio cities boomed as outside investors rushed to hitch their wagons to the region's rising star.

But by around 1890 it was apparent that the dream of a permanent flow of natural gas was just that. The older wells were starting to run dry. New wells were increasingly harder to find and, when they were found, lacked the volume and pressure of the original ones. The private pipelines built to bring gas to Toledo from Hancock County were enveloped in clouds of politics and accusations of price-gouging. A report issued by a state geologist in late 1890 warned that the gas fields were being "rapidly depleted." And a city of Toledo pipeline, built to compete against the private lines, that opened in 1891 became known more for its substantial debt than for any amounts of gas it delivered.

Within a few years the majority of industries in the area that had converted to natural gas had gone back to old and reliable coal. By this time gas, which had been hailed as an economic godsend, was now dismissed as an economic burden. The natural gas industry which entered northwest Ohio with such a roar had exited with a barely audible hiss.

But the era of fuel production in northwest Ohio was not over. There was still plenty of oil out there, oil that had been generally shunned during the region's brief but intense love affair with natural gas. One who had not shunned that black, oozy substance was oil baron John D. Rockefeller of Cleveland and his company, Standard Oil. Rockefeller had little interest in natural gas for he saw oil, and its ability to be stored in large tanks and transported and used when needed, as the fuel with the most long-term potential. By 1890, with its experience and capital, Standard Oil was a solid presence in northwest Ohio, having absorbed Findlay's Ohio Oil Company, now Marathon Oil, and built a major refinery in Lima.

During the next decade a forest of oil derricks sprouted in all the northwest Ohio counties with Wood County earning the reputation of "King of the Gusher." The southeastern townships of the county proved to be particularly productive and the sleepy village of Wayne, then called Prairie Depot, became a boom town practically overnight when a gusher was struck there in the spring of 1890. By the end of that year over 400 wells in and near the town were sucking black gold from deep beneath what had once been the Black Swamp.

The oil derricks were so thick in places in Prairie Depot that it was possible to step from one to the other without touching the ground. John D. Rockefeller himself was a frequent visitor to the town. And so many speculators and oil workers poured into town that some had to sleep in barns or open fields at night until housing could be built.

In typical boom town fashion, new businesses flocked to Prairie Depot: sawmills to supply wood for oil derricks and new housing; machine shops and welders to produce and re-pair tools; and boarding houses and saloons to house and feed oil workers flourished, to name a few.

The life of an oil worker was a rough one, both on and off the job. Falls from derricks and fires from natural gas were common. Highly volatile nitroglycerin which was used to "shoot" the well, that is make the final penetration through rock, at times went off in the wrong places taking life and limb. And when it was time to relax, hard drinking and bare-knuck-led brawling were not unusual pursuits.

Environmental concerns were virtually nonexistent and when a well was shot and a gusher followed, the homes and trees in Prairie Depot might be dripping with a spray of oil. Area creeks and streams frequently ran black with oil runoff which would be burned off by tossing flaming branches into them, the fires sometimes spreading into adjacent farm fields.

But these were minor concerns as there was oil to be drilled and money to be made. In the 1890's Wood County was be-lieved to be the greatest oil-producing county in the country. In May 1897 the *Toledo Daily Blade* noted "Wood County has always been the greatest oil producing section of Ohio. From a rough, swampy section of the state, where farms were plas-tered with mortgages, and a 160-acre tract a few years ago could scarcely be sold for taxes, has grown one of the wealthiest coun-ties in Ohio..."

The oil boom spread some gold Toledo's way even though little oil was found in or near the city, the same article pointed out. "Ten years ago it would have been difficult to have found ten men who could truthfully say they were each worth $100,000. Today they are legion... Every year several men who have made their fortunes in oil move to Toledo." And by 1900 Toledo could boast of four oil refineries, nearly 30 oil producers, and a half a dozen oil well supply companies.

Like natural gas, the northwest Ohio oil wells dried up, but at a much more deliberate pace. It's been a long time since an oil derrick towered over northwest Ohio. But in the oil refineries in Lima and Toledo and in Findlay's Marathon Oil Company, the legacy of black gold lives on.

Oil derricks tower over the town of Prairie Depot, now Wayne, in Wood County in 1892. (Photo courtesy of Wayne Public Library).

Chapter XIX:

A DICKENSIAN VIEW OF OHIO

The noted British author Charles Dickens came to America in 1842 both to see the cities on the East Coast and to sample the new frontier that had stretched to the Mississippi River. Afterward he published an account of his travels, *American Notes*. The book is not only highly entertaining but gives a unique view of a young United States of America as seen through the eyes of an observant and erudite visitor.

In addition, Dickens wrote regular letters throughout his journey describing his travels to John Forster back in England, his close friend and godfather to his children. While the letters contained much material similar to his book they also contained pithy and sometimes scathing observations of Americans he encountered, particularly those on the frontier. These observations were toned down considerably in his book. Forster published the letters written to him by Dickens in 1905. The letter detailing the Ohio leg of his journey was written by Dickens in Sandusky on April 24, 1842.

Dickens arrived in America at Boston in late January of 1842 and by mid-April had made it to St. Louis where he began his return trip East, a journey that would pass through northwest Ohio. Traveling with him was his wife and his personal secretary Mr. Q.

The party arrived in Columbus from Cincinnati April 21st and spent the night at the Neill House, a fine hotel with rooms

Dickens compared to those found in an Italian mansion. The next morning they left for their eventual destination of Sandusky. As the regular stagecoach did not run that day, Dickens chartered a private stage.

They began their journey on a corduroy road, a very rough road made by laying felled trees on marshland . "Good Heavens," Dickens wrote, "If only you felt one of the least of the jolts with which the coach falls from log to log!... Now the coach flung us on a heap on the floor and now crushed our heads against its roof. Now one side was deep in the mire and we were holding onto the other. Now it is laying on the horse tails, now again upon its own back."

Despite the rough start, Dickens enjoyed the trip. For the extra expense of chartering his own coach provided him a much needed break from folks that populated the further regions of the country at that time. "Still the day was beautiful, the air delicious," the author wrote. "And we were *alone* with no tobacco spittle or eternal prosy about dollars and politics (the only two subjects they ever converse about or can converse upon) to bore us." The group stopped for a picnic lunch of cold meats and wine, a fallen tree serving as their table, and continued on.

As evening began to fall the skies were lit by the vivid lightning of a spring thunderstorm and Dickens began to imagine various shapes he was seeing in the stumps of fallen trees that lined the road. "Now there is a Grecian urn erected in the center of a lonely field; now there is a woman weeping at a tomb; now a student poring over a book; now a horse, a dog, a cannon, an armed man; now a hunchback throwing off his cloak and stepping into the light..."

The coach arrived after 10 p.m. in Upper Sandusky, an old Wyandot Indian village with a few white residents. There they roused the sleeping operators of an inn, "a rough log house," to get accommodations. "We had the queerest sleeping room," Dickens penned, "with two doors one opposite the other both opening directly into the wild, black country and neither having any lock or bolt. The effect of these opposite doors was that one was always blowing the other open, an ingenuity in the art of building which I don't remember to having met with before."

This lack of security concerned Dickens greatly for he was traveling with a substantial amount of gold. He eventually succeeded in blockading the doors with his luggage and went to sleep. His secretary, Mr. Q, did not fare as well. "Mr. Q went to bed in the roof of the log house somewhere but was so beset by bugs that he got up after an hour and lay in the coach where he was obliged to wait until breakfast." Shivering in the cold, Mr. Q was kept awake all night by the squealing and grunting of pigs outside the coach.

The next morning "we breakfasted, driver and all, in one common room." Dickens wrote. "It was papered with newspapers and was as rough a place as need be." Also dining with them was a government Indian agent who was negotiating with local Indians for their removal west. "A kind old gentleman," Dickens reported, who "had witnessed many such removals and always with pain." And of American Indians in general Dickens concluded, "they are a fine people but degraded and broken down."

After breakfast the group left Upper Sandusky for the village of Tiffin. There they caught a train and arrived in Sandusky that evening. In Sandusky the Dickens party waited for a steamer to take them to Buffalo. They stayed "in a small house here but a very comfortable one." Dickens described the landlord as a "handsome, obliging, civil fellow. He comes into the room with his hat on; spits in the fire place as he talks; sits down on the sofa with his hat on; pulls out his newspaper and reads; but to all this I am accustomed. He is anxious to please—and that is enough."

As Dickens prepared to leave the American frontier behind he made in his Sandusky letter some general observations of his experience. Of the rudimentary monetary system he encountered he lamented over "the strange state of things in this country. It has no money, really *no money*. The bank paper won't pass; the newspapers are full of advertisements from tradesmen who sell by barter; and American gold is not to be had or purchased."

But Dickens strongest observations were saved for the people he encountered in his western journey. "Their demeanour in these country parts is invariably morose, sullen, clownish, and repulsive. I should think not, on the face of the earth, a people so entirely destitute of humour, vivacity, or the capacity of enjoyment. It is most remarkable."

The author was just getting warmed up. "I am quite serious when I say that I have not heard a hearty laugh these six weeks except my own; nor have I seen a merry face on any shoulders but a black man's. Lounging listlessly about, idling in barrooms; smoking, spitting; and lolling on the pavement in rocking chairs, outside the shop doors; are the only recreations. I don't think national shrewdness extends beyond the Yankees, that is, the Eastern men. The rest are heavy, dull, and ignorant."

Dickens concluded his Sandusky letter as the steamer arrived leaving him enough time to "swallow a hasty apology for dinner and hurry my train on board with all the speed I might." He made a seasick sailing to Buffalo on Lake Erie and spent a week at Niagara Falls on the English (Canadian) side where, awestruck by the falls, he was very much the giddy tourist.

Charles Dickens must have been quite happy to be back on native soil. For his next letter to John Forster written from there started "Niagara Falls!!! Upon the English side." The word English was underlined ten times.

Snapshots

1. WHERE TWO RIVERS MEET

"I defy the English, the Indians, and all the devils in Hell to take it," said General "Mad Anthony" Wayne of a high bluff above the confluence of the Maumee and Auglaize rivers in August, 1794. There he named the fort he built Defiance, his base of operations in the Battle of Fallen Timbers later that month and the beginning of the end for the Indians of the Maumee Valley.

While no trace of Fort Defiance remains, the site has been preserved in the city of Defiance, a quiet, locust tree shaded summit with a sweeping view. Below this tranquil bluff the waters of the Auglaize and Maumee rivers seamlessly blend on their long journey to the Atlantic Ocean.

The bluff rolls and dips a bit where the fort's foundations were dug. Scattered stone markers tell that the fort's gate was here, an Indian scout is buried there, while pointing toward the river two old cannons stand silent sentry. A wooden flagstaff rises where the fort's original one stood. A stone there tells that at one time all land north to Canada was surveyed on a baseline from that point.

Sharing the bluff a bit to the west is the Defiance Public Library, a Carnegie library built in 1904. Its walls of Mansfield Sandstone, a wavy lined stone of elegant hues of red, present a visual feast. While Anthony Wayne may have proclaimed this bluff a place of war over 200 years ago, it now is a most decidedly peaceful promontory.

A cannon points from a bluff at the confluence of the Maumee and Auglaize rivers in Defiance. General Anthony Wayne built Fort Defiance on this spot in 1794, his base of operations in the Battle of Fallen Timbers that year.

2. TURKEY FOOT ROCK

According to legend, Chief Turkey Foot of the Ottawa Indians stood atop this rock rallying his warriors during the Battle of Fallen Timbers in 1794. He was struck by a soldier's bullet and fell dead beside it. Some time after the battle members of his tribe made engravings in the rock in his homage, some of which can still be seen.

The rock moved around a bit before coming to its current resting place at the Fallen Timbers State Memorial in 1950. After lying somewhat ignored on a Maumee farm for a number of years, a group of Toledoans slipped into Maumee and stole it in 1899 thinking it would make a fine display for a state centennial celebration they hoped would be held in Toledo in 1903. Outrage immediately grew in that river town and the rock was quickly returned to the farm while Toledo's centennial celebration never materialized.

Chief Turkey Foot of the Ottawa Indians rallied his warriors from atop this rock during the Battle of Fallen Timbers before being felled by a soldier's bullet, according to legend. The rock lies adjacent to the Fallen Timbers Monument in Maumee.

3. ROCHE DE BOEUF

South of Waterville above the swirling rapids of the Maumee River rise two monuments, one natural, the other manmade; a great boulder known as Roche de Boeuf and the graceful arches of the old Ohio Electric Interurban Railway bridge. Roche de Boeuf, French for "Rock of Beef," may have been so named because Indians once had feasts there.

The ancient rock was also believed to be a meeting place for tribal councils over the centuries and it is said that General Anthony Wayne held his war council there the evening of August 19, 1794, the night before the Battle of Fallen Timbers which altered the history of the region.

Controversy reigned in the early 1900's when the railway company announced plans to build a bridge using the rock to anchor one of its piers. The Maumee Valley Pioneer Association talked of erecting a statue of Anthony Wayne on the rock and going to court if necessary to stop the railway's plans, but that never happened.

After the bridge was completed the now defunct *Toledo News-Bee* railed; "That historical and famous upriver landmark, Roche de Boeuf, has been practically obliterated by the construction of this bridge. All the glamour and beauty of this famous rock has been taken away by commercialism...Its beauty as a landmark is gone, and now, instead of towering out majestically at the head of the Rapids of the Miami, as it was wont to do during centuries past, it seems to be hiding its head in shame..."

It's likely that quite a few people at the time shared the newspaper's feelings and grandparents told their grandchildren of a time when the mighty rock stood alone in the river with no bridge looming over it.

The bridge, nearly a hundred years old now, has not been used in many years although its 12 arches spanning the river still serve as a subject for photographers and painters. It is crumbling and pieces of its concrete regularly tumble to the Maumee River. Someday the bridge will be gone and Roche de Boeuf will again stand alone, and grandparents will tell their grandchildren of the pretty, old railway bridge that once stood there.

The graceful arches of a former rail bridge
span the Maumee River and the boulder
Roche de Boeuf south of Waterville. The
rock is believed to have been a meeting
place for tribal councils.

4. THE LAST OTTAWA

Of all the Indian tribes that roamed the Maumee Valley the Ottawas were perhaps the most numerous. By the late 1830's virtually all of them had been forcibly removed west, save for a scattered group or family. One family that remained was that of Tee-na-beek who lived in the traditional Indian way near the village of Grand Rapids.

In the spring of 1850 he became seriously ill and died. Attending to him in his last days was Colonel Dresden Howard of Winameg, the noted friend of the area Indians. With no Native land left for Tee-na-beek to be buried, Howard laid him to rest in his family plot in Grand Rapids where his parents, grandparents and uncles lay.

In Howard's opinion Tee-na-beek was the last full-blooded Indian to be buried in the Maumee Valley. The Howard Cemetery, perched on a knoll above Grand Rapids, looks over the Maumee River and valley that was home to untold thousands of Indians at one time, an appropriate resting place for the last one.

The final resting place of Tee-Na-Beek in the Howard Cemetery, Grand Rapids. On the upper right hand corner of the stone is a shell filled with tobacco, a traditional offering frequently placed on Native graves.

5. THE PAUPERS FIELD

In the 1800's the movement toward county homes or poorhouses became popular. Their purpose was to house the aged, the disabled, the mentally ill, or anyone else who fell though the cracks of society and could not care for themselves.

In 1869 the Wood County Home opened, housing that county's needy. Many people spent their final days there, a cemetery on the property their final resting place. In the 1950's the grave markers were removed to ease maintenance and in 1971 the home was closed, assuring it seemed, those buried in the cemetery would be forever anonymous.

However in the early 1990's a movement began to restore the cemetery known as Sunset Acre and a number of local persons and groups became involved. The grave markers, which had ended up in various locations, were tracked down and reset. The cemetery was rededicated Memorial Day weekend, 1998.

It would have been easy to ignore an old graveyard filled with forgotten people who lived their final days on the fringe of society. But due to the remarkable effort of those involved, stone testament of their existence will live on.

The old county home, a sprawling Victorian complex, is now the Wood County Historical Museum and Center. Sunset Acre Cemetery is located on the grounds.

Sunset Acre Cemetery, located near Bowling Green.

6. TRAILMARKER TREE

Where the Portage River winds through Woodville stands a hulking, aged, hackberry tree. In the early 1800's, as the story goes, an Indian bent a branch in the tree to mark a shallow spot in the river and an easy crossing.

The broken branch grew, its 90 degree angle an unmistakable sign telling both Indians and the settlers that came later of a safe place to cross the river The tree is quite old now, its trunk in advanced stages of rot. Like the Indian who bent its branch when it was a young sapling, it too will become a part of history. The floodplain where the old tree stands is now a park, Trailmarker Park.

The aging Trailmarker Tree stands along the Portage River in Trailmarker Park in Woodville.

7. OLD BETSY

On a hill above downtown Fremont, site of the Birchard Public Library, sits an old cannon named Old Betsy. Its kindly-sounding name belies the death that roared from its mouth on an August day in 1813.

The hill was once the site of Fort Stephenson, a smallish War of 1812 fort. In late July, 1813, when the British and Indians had called off the second of two unsuccessful sieges of Fort Meigs, morale was plummeting and they desperately needed a win. Fort Stephenson, with only about 160 soldiers, seemed like easy pickings.

They arrived near the fort August 1st and the British opened up with field artillery and shells from gunboats anchored in the Sandusky River while the Indians poured in a steady stream of rifle fire. Fort Stephenson was led by a young major named George Croghan, only 21 years old, but wily beyond his years. He had but the one cannon, Old Betsy, which he move around to make the British and Indians think he had more. While the fort was small it was stoutly built, and the artillery barrage did little damage.

Late in the afternoon on August 2nd the British made their move and charged the fort. Major Croghan ordered his troops to sit tight and hold their fire while the cannon, which had been loaded with grapeshot and slugs, was wheeled into position. To reach the walls of the fort, the British had to pass through a low, dry moat. The Indians, for the most part, watched from a distance as they considered such tactics to be suicidal.

When the British were about 50 feet away a port hole in the fort opened and the cannon roared out its load of shrapnel while the rest of the American soldiers loosed a volley of rifle fire. Caught in the open moat, the British were literally shredded and the ones left standing ran for their lives. That evening the Indians withdrew and British dragged their wounded onto their boats and sailed back to Canada never to return to Ohio. Fort Stephenson suffered the loss of one soldier while British casualties were over 100.

On a hill above downtown Fremont on the onetime site of Fort Stephenson stands "Old Betsy."
With this single cannon the soldiers of the lightly
guarded fort repelled a vastly superior British
and Indian force on August 2, 1813.

About the Author:

JIM MOLLENKOPF is a free-lance writer and photographer from Toledo, Ohio, with a strong interest in local history. He was a social worker for 18 years, then a reporter for *The Review Times* newspaper in Fostoria, Ohio.

This is his second book. He wrote and published *Lake Erie Sojourn: An Autumn Tour of the Parks, Public Places, and History of the Lake Erie Shore*, in 1998.